SOME PRINCIPLES FOR

Evaluating Shorthand Systems

MARSDON ALEXANDER SHERMAN

*Submitted in partial fulfillment of the requirements for the
degree of Doctor of Philosophy, in the Faculty of Philosophy,
Columbia University*

King's Crown Press · Publishers
Morningside Heights · New York
1945

ACKNOWLEDGMENTS

The author wishes to express his appreciation to his sponsor, Professor Hamden L. Forkner, for his cooperation, guidance, helpful suggestions, and criticism, and to Professor Helen M. Walker and Dr. Thelma M. Potter for their helpful suggestions and criticisms.

Acknowledgments are due to Dr. Jane Dorsey Zimmerman for her counseling and assistance in the phases of this study dealing with phonetics, to Raymond Hodges for his contribution to the phonetic word list used in this study, and to Nadia Danilevsky for her suggestions on the statistical phases of this study.

Acknowledgments are also due to Mrs. Jacqueline E. Hodges and to Edith-Gene Sherman, the author's wife, for their aid in the clerical phases of the study.

Finally, acknowledgments are due to the thirteen authors and writers of the several shorthand systems who so generously gave of their time and effort in order to furnish the data required in the word sample.

M.A.S.

TABLE OF CONTENTS

List of Tables

SOME PRINCIPLES FOR EVALUATING SHORTHAND SYSTEMS

CHAPTER 1

THE PROBLEM, ITS IMPORTANCE, AND A DESCRIPTION OF PRESENT-DAY SHORTHAND SYSTEMS

For many years authors and writers of shorthand have been voicing claims concerning the superiority of one system of shorthand over another. Studies have been made in an attempt to prove the advantages of one specific system over another specific system, but in no instance has an objective basis been established by which shorthand systems can be universally evaluated.

I. THE PROBLEM

Statement of the Problem

The purpose of this study is to isolate some of the factors which enter into the reading and writing of manually written shorthand systems, and, by considering these factors, to establish criteria for the objective evaluation of shorthand systems with respect to their facility of reading and writing.

Delimitation of the Study

Shorthand is itself a highly complex method of recording spoken sounds. Many factors must enter into the problems of learning to write, to read, and to transcribe shorthand notes. Various methods might be undertaken to establish principles for the evaluation of a system. This study is concerned only with certain characteristics, namely, the structural characteristics which make up the system and the judgment factors which enter into the reading of the system. No attempt is made to evaluate the complex problems of learning a shorthand system, inasmuch as learning depends upon many variables such as language background of the student, the interest of the student, the proficiency of the teacher, the effectiveness of materials of instruction, and the maturity of the student, to name only a few.

Definition of Terms

<u>Shorthand system</u>: A form of abbreviated writing which uses the
known letters of the alphabet and/or symbols representing
speech sounds.

<u>Structural characteristics</u>: Those factors which enter into
  (a) the writing of a shorthand system and are measured by the
      number of strokes required to express speech sounds,
      which when combined form words. A stroke is defined as
      a straight line, a curve, a circle, a loop, a hook, or
      a pen-lift. Example: /,), o, 0, u, / o.
  (b) the reading of a shorthand system which is measured by
      the extent to which a word in a shorthand system is
      complete in representing speech sounds of the word.

<u>Judgment factor</u>: The degree to which one must exercise judg-
ment to determine the correct word from among one or more
choices. If, for example, a certain symbol in a shorthand
system stands for more than one word, a judgment factor must
enter into the correct reading of the word. The greater the
number of judgment factors, the less efficient the system.

Importance of the Study

At the present time there are a large number of shorthand
systems taught in the public and private schools of the United
States. Examples of some of the current systems of shorthand
are: Abernethy (1)*, American (27), Byrne (7), Capitol (29),
Dickinson (13), Direction (18), Garber's International (22),
Gregg (24), Hyenga (26), Isaac Pitman (30), Munson (15), Myers
(28), Phonetic (10), Rowe Shorthand (31), Script (12), Shamburger (36), Speedhand (8), Speedscript (33), Spencerian (37),
Stautzenberger (38), Thomas Natural (40), and Universal (41).

An indication of the extent of the use of these shorthand
systems is shown in the following statements taken from literature of the various publishers of shorthand systems.

"Gregg shorthand is taught in 6,519 cities and towns -- more

* The numbers in parentheses represent bibliographical references (pages
55-57).

than 97 percent of the public schools that teach shorthand "
(24:vii).

Isaac Pitman Shorthand reports that the Pitman system is over-
whelmingly preferred in eight out of the ten largest cities in
the English-speaking world -- New York, London, Chicago, Phila-
delphia, Sydney, Glasgow, Birmingham, and Melbourne (42).

In a report issued along with a pamphlet by the author of
Thomas Natural Shorthand, it is stated that from 1934 to 1939
the number of schools in California teaching Natural Shorthand
increased from 100 to 700 percent. A list, dated April 1, 1940,
and distributed with the pamphlet, shows that twenty-one schools
consisting of high schools, junior colleges, and colleges have
adopted Natural Shorthand in California. Testimonial letters
contained in the pamphlet show that it is taught in other states
as well (32).

The Speedscripter, a paper issued by the publishers of Speedscript Shorthand, lists twelve business colleges, located from
Tennessee to Massachusetts, which would offer Speedscript dur-
ing the summer of 1943 (39).

Many other systems are taught in private schools of the United
States as well as public schools. Some are taught in private
classes conducted in the home of the author. Universal Shorthand
and Phonetic are among the systems taught in the homes of their
authors.

In the literature distributed by authors and publishers, each
system claims a superiority over all other systems. The systems
are usually reported to be easier to learn, faster to write,
and more accurately read than any other system. For example:
The New Standard Course in Pitman Shorthand states that its purpose is "to reduce materially the time occupied in learning ele-
mentary principles of stenography" (30:iii-iv).

The Anniversary Edition of Gregg Shorthand sums up its advantages by saying:

Gregg Shorthand may be learned in from one-third to one-
half the time required by the old systems. Gregg Shorthand is
the most legible shorthand in existence. The easy, natural
appearance of the writing in Gregg Shorthand appeals to every
impartial investigator...the system has greater speed possi-
bilities than any other system (24:vii).

Thomas says of Natural Shorthand:

Because of the simplicity, legibility, and speed of the system, the use of Thomas Natural Shorthand lightens the shorthand learning load,... (40:vi).

Garber's International Shorthand is a complete and original system designed to meet the requirements for accuracy and speed in the reproduction of any spoken word (22:1).

The outstanding features of Hyenga Shorthand are its reading power, legibility, and speed (26:1).

Byrne Simplified Shorthand is complete, thorough, accurate, legible, and rapid (7:1).

This system can be learned as quickly and easily as any system in use. It is as rapid as human speech, and is more easily written and read than any other system of real shorthand published (1:1). The foregoing statement is made by the author of Abernethy Curve-Stroke Shorthand.

There have been a number of studies (3, 6, 9) conducted which attempted to determine the superiority of one system over another, but each of these studies was limited to a comparison of only one system of shorthand with another. Studies are frequently difficult to conduct and difficult to control where comparative groups of students are used, and when completed, they have findings on only two systems of shorthand to the exclusion of all the remaining shorthand systems.

The last "Biennial Survey of Education in the United States" in which shorthand was reported is for 1934-36. It reports that there were in excess of 400,000 students studying shorthand in this country in 1936 (4). It is therefore reasonable to believe that a study aimed at determining the most efficient shorthand system is one of sufficient importance to warrant its being made.

Possible Educational Implications

One study (20) reports that the percentage of failures in shorthand runs well over 50 percent. This high percentage of failures maintains in spite of the fact that great strides have been taken to improve shorthand teaching methods. The fact that failures persist emphasizes the need for a method of evaluation which can be universally applied to all manually written short-

hand systems in order to discover the most efficient system
which may be made available to schools and students of shorthand. Thus one of the possible causes of failure in shorthand
would be minimized. Also, in the process of evaluation, certain
characteristics in the now existing shorthand systems may be
discovered and studied which would eventually lead to the development of a system more efficient than any of the present
systems.

Aside from failure in shorthand, there is the fact that
400,000 students are studying shorthand. It is of the greatest
educational and economic importance that they have at their
disposal the most efficient of the many systems now in existence so that they may realize, as nearly as possible, their
greatest potential of achievement. As a result of the present
study there will be a means for evaluating systems of shorthand
with regard to certain efficiency factors. When the findings of
this study are applied to existing systems, it will give super-
intendents and school boards a means of choosing a more efficient system of shorthand for their schools.

In evaluating shorthand systems by the method presented in
this study, it is possible to determine weaknesses as well as
strengths in a system. A teacher who is aware of the weaknesses
in the system he is teaching may vary his teaching methods in
order to emphasize the efforts of the students on those weak
phases and thus overcome them or balance them. On the other
hand, a teacher may stress the strong phases so that they will
offset the disadvantages of the weaknesses. For example: If a
system is inefficient in writing, a teacher can stress the necessity of becoming highly proficient in writing the system and
place less stress upon other phases which are more efficient;
or if a system is highly efficient in the reading phase, a
teacher can emphasize the reading phase to develop skill sufficient to overcome other inefficiencies of a system.

II. PRESENT-DAY SHORTHAND SYSTEMS

Characteristics of Shorthand Systems Being Used Today

As a preliminary part of this study, an examination was made
of some twenty-one existing systems of shorthand. This prelimi-

nary study was concerned with general characteristics of both manually and machine written systems. As a result of this pre-liminary study, it was discovered that the systems could be classified under three major categories.

1. <u>Machine written shorthand</u>
   a. Those systems which use combinations of printed let-ters to make up words written by the use of a machine, such as the Stenotype and Stenograph shorthand systems.

Example:	S K W R	E					Gentlemen:
			F P L T			)	
			F P L T			) colon	
	K W R					Why	
	TK	O				do	
	W	E				we	
	T P H	O		T		not	
	H	E R				hear	
	T P R	U				from you	
	T P H					in	
	R	E				re-	
	TKPW A	R		D		gard	
	T	O U R				to your	
	PW	EU	L			bill	
	ST P H					question mark	

2. <u>A shortened form of longhand</u>
   a. Shorthand systems which use regular longhand letters in combination with shorthand symbols. These systems are manually written.
   Example: (Speedwriting)

   Translation: Gentlemen: Why do we not hear from you
      in regard to your bill?

3. Character or symbol writing
   a. Those systems which use symbols independent of long-hand. Each symbol represents a phonetic sound or combina-tion of sounds, and these symbols are combined to form words. Such systems as Gregg and Isaac Pitman shorthand are in this category.

Example: (Gregg)

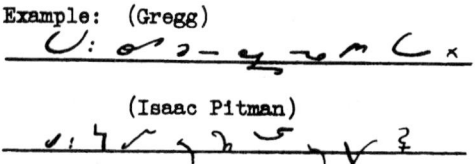

(Isaac Pitman)

Translation: Gentlemen: Why do we not hear from you
in regard to your bill?

Of the character- or symbol-writing types of shorthand there
are two further subdivisions. The characters have evolved into
two distinct types. Some systems made their characters conform
to a geometric design of straight lines, circles, and arcs.
They are usually classified as geometric systems. Isaac Pitman
Shorthand falls in this classification (see example above).

Other systems have taken on the characteristics of our
present-day longhand script, using elliptical curves and
straight lines. A system such as Gregg is classified in this
category; it has been classified as a cursive shorthand system
(see example above).

Among these systems of symbol- or character-writing there
have developed a number of methods of expressing sounds. These
methods of expressing sounds are varied among the several systems. This is accomplished by such devices as position and
and shading.

In a shorthand system which uses position writing, such as
Isaac Pitman, the vowel sound changes by writing a single character in several positions with respect to the line of writing.
The vowel is therefore omitted from the writing of the outline.
The vowel is expressed by the position in which the consonant
is written. The position-writing systems vary in the number of
positions employed from two to five positions.

Example: (Isaac Pitman, a position system)

\ ĕp   \ ăp   \ ĭp

(Gregg, a non-position system)

ʃ ĕp   ʃ ăp   ʃ ĭp

Position-writing as used by Isaac Pitman refers to the common
practice among several shorthand systems of using the placement

of characters for the purpose of indicating vowel sounds. The
systems which are classified as non-position systems are, in
fact, not entirely free from position writing. Certain prefixes
and suffixes are written with a definitely defined position.
Definitions are also given to direct the writing of an outline.
For example: Gregg says that the first consonant of an outline
should be written on the line. It can also be said that any
system in which various lengths of lines are used necessitates
the use of position in that the writer must consider the point
at which the character or outline must be started in order to
have it placed properly in relation to the line of writing. A
thorough examination of samples submitted by authors and writ
ers reveals this statement to be true with regard to each of
the systems in the samples, some of which claim to be non-
position systems.

Example:

Longhand Word	*	System Number					
	1	2	3	4	5	6	7
asked							
beach							
	8	9	10	11	12	13	14
asked							
beach							

It will be noted that, in every instance, there is reference to
a line of writing even though that reference has varying degrees of interpretation. Inasmuch as this factor is common to
all systems, it is not considered to be a factor of efficiency.

A shorthand system in which shading is used, for example
Isaac Pitman, varies the intensity of sound by the use of
shaded or light lines. By using both shading and position, a
single character can be made to express a large number of
sounds.

Example: (Isaac Pitman)

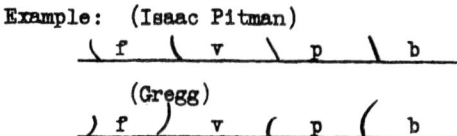

(Gregg)

In a light line system, such as Gregg, which claims not to use position, all of the essential sounds are written into the outline or character.

Example:

As the result of the preliminary study mentioned above, it was discovered that the systems are distributed in the following manner among the above-mentioned categories.

1. Nine systems are of the so-called non-position type. Twelve systems use position-writing to express certain letters or sounds.

    a. One uses two positions.

    b. Seven use three positions.

    c. Two use four positions.

    d. Two use five positions.

2. Authors reported that vowels are fully written in ten systems, partially written in eight, and no vowels are written in the remaining three systems.

3. Eight systems use shading in writing to express intensity of sound, while thirteen do not.

4. Nine systems use longhand letters in writing.

    a. Four systems use the entire longhand letters in writing.

    b. Five use only part of the longhand letter.

    c. Twelve authors claimed their outlines are independent of any part of longhand.

5. Two systems are machine-written systems.

6. It was found that twelve systems of shorthand are cursive, while nine are geometric in form.

CHAPTER 2

REVIEW OF THE LITERATURE

Data pertaining to evaluation of shorthand systems consist
largely of statements by authors and publishers, results of national speed contests, results of students' achievement in
Regent's examinations in the State of New York, and, finally,
results of comparative studies made in an attempt to prove the
superiority of one shorthand system over another. All of the
last mentioned type of studies have been conducted upon the
group-comparison method of research and therefore are related
to this study only in that they were attempting to evaluate
shorthand systems. Since the above-mentioned studies approach
their evaluation from an entirely different point of view, only
enough of these studies will be reviewed here to exemplify
their approach in contrast to the approach of this study.

National Contests for Shorthand Writers

At one time national contests were conducted for speed writers in shorthand. Such contests were held by the National
Shorthand Reporters Association, and speeds from 200 to 282
words a minute with accuracy ratings running from 98.32 to
99.81 percent are reported for writers of Gregg Shorthand (24:
ix). An Isaac Pitman writer in the National Shorthand Reporters Association contest of 1922 reached a speed of 349 words
per minute for two minutes (42). These contests were based upon
the achievements of a few individuals, and their results may
have been due more to individual aptitude than to a superior or
less superior system of shorthand. At any rate, there could be
little scientific basis for a statement concerning the superiority of one system over another on the results made by the limited number of contestants.

Regents' Examinations in New York State

Another comparison of shorthand systems might have been based on the Regent's examinations for New York State. In the public schools of New York City both Gregg and Isaac Pitman shorthand are taught. The number of pupils who failed in each system might have offered criteria for presuming that the superior system would have the least failures in the Regents' examinations. The limitations are, however, that it would be a means of evaluating only the two systems of shorthand taught in the New York City schools.

Studies Evaluating Shorthand Systems

In 1940 a study was made by Brady (6) which undertook to compare beginning shorthand students' performance in Thomas Natural Shorthand and in Gregg Shorthand. The study was conducted with a class of fourteen beginning Gregg Shorthand students and seventeen Thomas Natural Shorthand students. At the time the final evaluation was made there remained only ten of the original Gregg students and fourteen Thomas students.

The study was conducted upon the group-comparison method and the groups were equated on the basis of their scores made on an intelligence test, English grades, typewriting grades, penmanship, age, sex, Strong's Vocational Interest Blank, and home background. Based on class achievement records, the study is reported to have shown a difference in favor of Thomas Natural Shorthand students.

Osborne Garber (21) made an outline of the characteristics of four systems of shorthand in which he attempted to compare his own system, International, with Thomas Natural, Gregg, and Isaac Pitman shorthand. No clue is given as to the sources of his investigation except that it is based on one thousand most frequently used words and the instruction manual for each system. He compared the four systems of shorthand on sixteen items. Among them are the average number of strokes per word, longhand movements, light line or shaded, positions used, two-way motions, easy joining, retracing or jogging, perpendicular strokes, word signs, phonetics, vowel markings, vowels, memory aids, dictionary, phrasing, and use in court reporting. Garber's analysis is a description of the characteristics of the four systems rather than an attempt to point out which is the best system. No explanation is given concerning the methods or materials used in his analysis.

M. Elinor Betts (3) submitted a Master's thesis to the University of Pittsburgh in 1942 which was entitled, "A Comparative Study of the Time Required for Development of Speed in Gregg Shorthand and Speedscript Shorthand." Her study was conducted with high school students. Of those students who remained to complete the theory and 80-word dictation, ninety-eight were Gregg while 133 were Speedscript students. Of those who still remained in the 90-word dictation, eighty-nine were Gregg while ninety-seven were Speedscript students. Of those who remained to complete the 100-word dictation, seventy-eight were Gregg while eighty-two were Speedscript students. The criteria upon which Betts based her comparison of the two systems of shorthand are:

1. The date on which each student began his study of shorthand theory.

2. The date on which he completed his study of theory, as determined by his passing the final theory tests.

3. The date on which he passed the 80-word dictation speed test.

4. The date on which he passed the 90-word dictation speed test.

5. The date on which he passed the 100-word dictation speed test.

6. The number of days on which he was absent from school between the time of his beginning theory and the time of his passing the 100-word test.

7. The system of shorthand which he used.

Betts' conclusions are that it takes the "average" Gregg Shorthand student thirty-five days longer to learn the theory of Gregg Shorthand than it does the Speedscript students to learn the theory of Speedscript.

The majority of Gregg students who were included in the complete study spent seventy-five school days in theory; the majority of the Speedscript students spent forty days in theory. And further, ... the actual range in days required from the end of theory to one hundred words a minute was twenty-seven to 286 for the Gregg group and forty-five to 178 for the Speedscript group. The median number of days for the two groups -- 91.04 for Gregg, 92.58 for Speedscript -- shows a difference of no significance (3).

One of the most complete and extensive comparative shorthand studies thus far made is the study of Script and Gregg shorthand conducted by Walter L. Deemer and Phillip J. Rulon (9). This study is a comparison of Script Shorthand and Gregg Shorthand, and was started in 1938 and concluded in 1941 at a cost of $50,000. The problem and conclusions as expressed in a summary of the shorthand study are:

> The purpose of the Shorthand Study was to determine the relative merits of Gregg and Script Shorthand when taught in public high schools for a period of two years, with the objective of general office use. In terms of the features examined in the study, Script Shorthand exhibited substantially greater relative merits (9:266).

Weaknesses in Former Studies

As a result of the claims made by the authors or publishers upon the superiority of their various shorthand systems, and through examination of the structural characteristics of shorthand, it was decided that shorthand could be compared quantitatively in areas of memory-burden, writing efficiency, and reading accuracy.

The claims of authors, as quoted in Chapter I of this study, are that their systems are easier to learn, faster to write, and more accurately read back. The last two factors mentioned cover the function of shorthand in that its usefulness consists in being able to record the spoken word rapidly and to reproduce it accurately in its original content at a later time.

The first claim, that of learning, has caused previous studies to be questioned. Learning brings in the relation of shorthand to the individual using it and also brings in the variable of individual differences which cannot be measured without using experimental groups of individuals.

There are two weaknesses in comparing shorthand systems by means of the experimental group method. First, nothing has yet been found which correlates highly enough with shorthand success

to enable groups to be properly equated upon that basis (5).
An adequate sample of individuals cannot be taken for comparative groups because of the limited basis upon which students
of the less popular shorthand systems are distributed throughout the country. In addition to the number of students being
limited, there is a greater limitation of numbers of teachers
of different systems. Many of the present-day systems are
taught only in the private business school of the inventor, or,
in some instances, they are taught to individuals or private
classes in the homes of their authors. The problem of equating
teachers' ability to teach shorthand has a significant bearing
on a study designed to compare facility of learning in a system.
Second, the experimental-group basis, because of the above-
mentioned limitations of teachers and pupils, excludes all but
a few systems in a study, and it is the purpose of this study
to establish principles of evaluation which can be applied to
all systems.

An example of the limitations of the group-experiment method
of evaluation for shorthand systems is clearly shown in the
Deemer-Rulon study (9:4) in which it was hoped that Isaac Pitman could be included in the study for the reason that Gregg
and Pitman are considered the two outstanding English-language
systems of the present day. In practice, however, it proved
impossible to get a sufficient number of Pitman classes to
give any assurance of statistically significant results.

Conclusions

None of the above studies presents conclusive evidence to
prove which of the many existing systems of shorthand is the
best. With the exception of the investigation by Garber (21),
which includes Isaac Pitman, International, Thomas Natural, and
Gregg Shorthand (see discussion, page 11), all of the other
studies are studies of only two systems of shorthand.

There is an apparent need for a study sufficiently broad to
be able to include all of the systems of shorthand, a study
which will be sufficiently scientific to be acceptable to those
who seek to know the best system of shorthand. The validity of
all of the studies thus far has been questioned on the basis of
equating of groups, validity of sample, teacher selection,

materials, and methods used in teaching. The human element
makes the factors of research so variable that none of the
findings are conclusive enough to outweigh completely criticism
of the errors of sampling, selection, and teaching methods.

In the present study the factors of comparison are based upon
the structural characteristics of shorthand in such a manner as
to eliminate uncontrollable individual differences which are
present when persons are being brought into a study. This sim-
plifies the study into a problem of establishing formulas for
evaluating structural characteristics and judgment factors of
shorthand systems.

CHAPTER 3

ESTABLISHING PRINCIPLES FOR EVALUATING CERTAIN EFFICIENCY FACTORS OF SHORTHAND SYSTEMS

Examination of Shorthand Systems

As a first step in establishing principles for evaluating shorthand systems, it was necessary to make a thorough study of as many existing systems as possible. A cursory study was made by the author of twenty-one shorthand systems in order to discover the characteristic similarities and differences among the several systems. As a result of this study, it was discovered that these shorthand systems have certain common characteristics which can be measured quantitatively.

The next step was to test this hypothesis. As a result of this cursory examination, it was possible to make certain tentative assumptions.

Assumptions

1. A shorthand system in which any character always represents the same word or phrase is more efficient than a system in which each character stands for more than one word.

2. A shorthand system in which there is a minimum of writing movements is more efficient than a system in which writing movements are numerous. A system using only one stroke for each word would be considered an ideal system. It is true that strokes vary in length and shape among the several shorthand systems, but it is further assumed that these differences tend to cancel out. This assumption is strengthened by a statement in The Handwriting Movement by Freeman (19) in which he says:

Long strokes are made with greater speed than short strokes, with the result that strokes widely differing in length may be made in the same or nearly the same length of time...

3. A shorthand system whose outlines completely express the longhand sounds is more efficient than a system in which the sounds are abbreviated.

4. A shorthand system should provide greater efficiency for writing high-frequency words than it does for writing low-frequency words.

5. All shorthand systems use position.

To test these tentative assumptions and to establish a basis for the development of factors of efficiency, a comprehensive survey was made of fourteen systems of shorthand now in current use.

In order to have a common basis for the establishment of the evaluating principles, it was necessary to select an adequate and representative sample of common English words which could be used as a basis for comparison throughout the study. This sample of common English words is included in Appendix C, and, for the purpose of insuring uniformity in evaluation, the phonetic spelling of each word is presented. This phonetic spelling conforms to the pattern of general American speech. The sound of each letter is represented by the key included with the word sample.

Methods and Reasons for Selecting the Word Sample

It is obviously impossible to include every word in the English language in such a study. It is also evident that the frequency of use of words is an important factor in applying any formula which seeks to measure the efficiency of a shorthand system. For example: The word "contract" occurs in use, according to Horn's Basic Writing Vocabulary (25), almost six times as frequently as the word "die." It is therefore necessary to take into account that a system of shorthand which uses an extremely complex outline for "contract" as compared to a system which uses an extremely simple outline is a less efficient system. In the case of the word "die," which is a word of lower frequency, the complexity or simplicity of the outline becomes much less important.

Inasmuch as all the words in the language would make the study too cumbersome, and inasmuch as frequency of use of words is an important factor, it was decided to use an adequate and representative sample of words selected from a generally accepted semantic study. A Basic Writing Vocabulary -- 10,000 Words Most Commonly Used in Writing by Ernest Horn (25) was chosen. This vocabulary was compiled from a study of 5,136,816 running words taken from the vocabularies of business correspondence; of personal letters from all parts of the country, including the vocabulary of letters of people of more than average literary ability; of well-known writers; of letters printed in magazines and metropolitan newspapers; of minutes, resolutions, and committee reports; and excuses written to teachers by parents (25:41).

Barnhart (2) reported that three thousand words constitute 97 percent of the ordinary dictation material. Dewey (11), in his study, "Relativ Frequency of English Speech Sounds," reported that the one thousand commonest words, in a study of one hundred thousand words which he made, will form over 75 percent of the material in any representative specimen of connected English. That these statements are accepted is shown by the fact that such books as Correlated Dictation and Transcription by Forkner, Osborne, and O'Brien (17) and 5,000 Most Used Shorthand Forms by Gregg based their vocabularies upon Horn's high-frequency words. Gregg says of his book of five thousand words, "... the pupil will have a writing vocabulary of more than 90 percent of all that he is likely to be called upon to write" (16).

Horn's first three thousand words were chosen for this study, because, as indicated above, they substantially represent the average dictation material and because they are a representative group of words upon which to measure the various systems of shorthand.

To compare all the shorthand systems using the entire list of three thousand words is neither practical nor necessary, provided an adequate representative sample of the three thousand words is selected. Therefore, a random sample was taken of the first three thousand words in Horn's list. The random sample was chosen in the following manner:

1. The three thousand words indicated as having the highest frequency in Horn's list were arranged alphabetically and numbered consecutively.

2. The sample was to be submitted to authors and expert writers of the several shorthand systems in order to obtain the data to be used in the investigation. Therefore, in

deciding upon the size of the sample to be taken, two factors
had to be considered:

a. If the sample were too large, the authors and writers
might have neither the time nor the desire to participate
in the study.

b. If the sample were too small, it might not be acceptable as a fair representation of the original three thousand words.

Sources of the Word Sample

Since it was evident that frequency of use of a word was to
be an important factor in objectively establishing efficiency
factors, three different random samples were taken of the three
thousand words. The first sample taken was an over-all sample
of the three thousand words. This sample consisted of five hundred words.

Inasmuch as the first five hundred words of highest frequency
represent a high proportion of all words used as compared to
the sixth five hundred words in the three thousand, it was decided to take two additional samples, one consisting of seventy
words from the first five hundred and another of seventy words
from the sixth five hundred. This was done for the purpose of
determining whether or not there would be a significant difference in efficiency factors of words of high frequency as compared to words of low frequency. These three samples represent
the over-all sample of five hundred words, the seventy words
from the first five hundred words, and the seventy words from
the sixth five hundred words -- a total of 640 words.

In selecting a random sample of a part of an over-all sample,
some duplications could be expected to occur. This did happen
in the case of twenty-six words, which left a net sample of 614
different words finally selected on which to make an analysis.

3. The process of choosing the five hundred over-all random
word sample from the list of three thousand words was accomplished in the following manner: Numbers were read off down
the columns of a list of random numbers (14) and correspond-
ing numbers on the list of three thousand words were checked
until five hundred of the three thousand words had been
checked off the list. Since zero occasionally appeared as one

or more of the four digits, it can be readily seen how the sample ran through the entire list of three thousand words.

Example: Encountering 07 97 (actually one of the numbers) in the list of random numbers meant that when the three thousand words were arranged alphabetically and numbered consecutively starting with the "a's," the 797th word was checked off as one of the words to become part of the five hundred word random sample to be taken. The number 00 11 (actually one of the numbers) meant that the eleventh word in the original list of three thousand words should be checked off to become part of the random sample of five hundred words.

4. The next step was to arrange the first five hundred highest frequency words of the list of three thousand in alphabetical order and number them consecutively. A random sample was then taken in the same manner as explained in step No. 3. This time, however, only three digits were used from the list of random numbers, as all numbers of five hundred or less can be represented by three digits. Seventy words were chosen as a random sample of the five hundred high-frequency words.

5. The procedure followed in step No. 4 was identical to that used in choosing the seventy word sample from the five hundred least frequently used words of Horn's first three thousand words.

6. The three samples consisting of 614 different words plus twenty-six repetitions were then combined without distinction on a twelve-page list to be sent to the authors and writers of various shorthand systems.

In applying the processes of evaluation in this study, the entire composite sample of 614 words was used as representative of the three thousand words. The result of adding seventy more words each from the first and last groups of five hundred words had little more effect than to add 114 additional random words to an already existing random sample. It tended to emphasize, slightly, the high- and low-frequency words of the original three thousand word list. Using the 614 words did, however, have three advantages:

1. It gave as complete a coverage for the three thousand words as could be obtained with the random sample words available.

2. It insured the inclusion, in the sample representing the three thousand words, of the words which had been canceled because of repetition.

3. It insured a higher return from authors and writers than a sample of one thousand words or more.

The two random samples of seventy words each, which represented the five hundred high-frequency and five hundred low-frequency words, were treated individually in the processes of evaluation in the study.

Application of the Word Sample

The next step in the study was to arrange the sample of 614 words, which included the three samples mentioned above, so that they could be sent to the authors or expert writers of the various shorthand systems. This was done by arranging the longhand words in a column and leaving two blank columns for the writers to fill in according to instructions (see Appendix B). Examples were given at the head of the column, and a letter of explanation (see Appendix A) was included, which also contained examples of the information needed.

This material was sent to twenty-two authors and expert writers of the several shorthand systems. Of these twenty-two sets of material sent out, fourteen were returned. Six sets were filled out completely for all three principles of evaluation, all fourteen were filled out for the principle of writing efficiency, eight supplied information on the word-completeness or reading-efficiency principle, and ten furnished complete information on the memory-burden or homonymetic-intensity principle.

Reasons for choosing the twenty-two persons to whom the random sample of words was sent were:

1. It was felt that an investigation on evaluation of shorthand systems would affect the author of a system most significantly, and it would seem best to allow him to participate in the study whenever possible. Of the fourteen people who participated in filling out the samples of this study, all were authors except in the case of Isaac Pitman Shorthand, Gregg Shorthand, and Munson Shorthand. The material of Isaac Pitman Shorthand was prepared by an expert Pitman writer, the material on Gregg Shorthand was completed by the author of

the present study, and the material on Munson Shorthand was sent to the publishers who submitted it to a writer of their system.

2. The manner in which the twenty-two systems were chosen for this study was as follows: The cursory survey mentioned above involved the sending of letters to seventy-five authors and publishers of the several shorthand systems. Answers were received from twenty-six authors and publishers, and as a result of a subsequent survey of these twenty-six shorthand systems it was found that twenty-one seemed anxious to impart information about their shorthand systems. Since this study is not, primarily, an evaluation of shorthand systems, it was not considered necessary to include every available and existing system of shorthand, and therefore the fourteen systems which finally sent in the necessary information were deemed adequate for the purposes of investigation.

The returns from this comprehensive survey indicate the following:

1. Many words within one system have the same outline. A complete analysis of the data collected through this survey is shown in Table I (page 23).

Table I indicates that shorthand systems vary with respect to the characteristic of homonyms. That is, the systems vary among themselves to a greater or less degree according to the number of outlines which stand for more than one word. Because of this variance among the systems, it is conceivable that there must be a variance of efficiency with respect to that characteristic in relation to the amount of that characteristic existing within a shorthand system.

A student using a system containing homonyms must either remember the word dictated, which results in added memory-burden, or he must review all the meanings of the outline and exercise a choice as to the correct one, or deduce its proper meaning from the content of the material in which it is placed. This necessitates an exercise of judgment. A shorthand system having no homonyms would be most efficient in that the necessity of memory-burden or the use of judgment would be eliminated.

2. There is a marked difference between the number of writing movements required for the same word by the various sys-

tems. Table II (page 24) shows the data collected through this survey in this respect. Tables II and III are based on a random sample of twenty-four words since it was a sufficient number of words to exemplify the point under discussion.

Table I

Number of Outlines Which Stand for More Than One Word

Shorthand System	Number of Meanings						
	1	2	3	4	5	6	7
1	368	148	59	28	9	1	1
2	442	129	37	6			
3	498	102	14				
4	457	129	24	4			
5	614						
6	393	190	31				
7	561	53					
8	441	105	47	16	5		
9	422	166	30	3	3		
10	No data						
11	No data						
12	No data						
13	510	59	44	1			
14	No data						

The table is read thus: Shorthand system No. 1 has 368 outlines in a random sample of 614 words which stand for only one word; it has 148 outlines which stand for two words, fifty-nine which stand for three words, twenty-eight which stand for four words, nine which stand for five words, one which stands for six words, and one which stands for seven words.

Table II

Number of Movements Required to Write the Same Word
in the Several Systems of Shorthand
Included in This Study

Word	Shorthand System													
	1	2	3	4	5	6	7	8	9	10	11	12	13	14
abroad	2	3	4	2	5	3	4	2	5	3	2	2	3	4
article	3	5	3	2	7	4	4	3	4	4	3	3	3	3
approximately	6	6	7	6	5	5	5	6	5	6	6	6	5	9
beautiful	3	3	3	3	5	3	4	2	4	3	3	3	4	7
capacity	4	5	5	5	5	5	4	5	5	4	4	4	5	6
climate	3	4	5	5	6	6	6	2	6	4	3	3	2	3
date	2	2	2	2	2	3	2	1	1	1	1	1	1	5
drive	3	3	4	2	4	2	3	2	4	3	3	3	4	4
favorite	3	3	3	3	5	4	3	2	5	5	6	3	2	4
further	2	2	3	2	4	3	4	2	2	4	3	1	5	2
helped	3	5	5	4	7	4	5	4	6	3	3	2	5	6
inquiry	4	5	5	3	4	2	4	4	3	4	3	4	5	7
later	1	3	3	2	5	2	4	1	4	3	2	1	3	7
manufacturers	5	5	5	4	5	6	8	5	4	6	7	5	8	10
more	2	2	1	2	2	1	2	1	1	2	2	2	3	4
omitted	2	7	4	4	6	6	4	4	4	3	3	2	4	5
piano	2	4	3	3	6	5	3	3	6	7	2	2	2	7
providing	5	6	5	4	9	6	5	3	6	3	4	5	5	8
remark	2	3	5	5	6	3	4	3	2	3	5	2	5	7
saying	2	4	3	4	3	4	4	2	4	4	2	2	4	4
shock	2	2	3	2	4	3	3	3	3	4	3	2	2	5
suffer	3	2	2	2	5	4	3	2	2	4	4	3	4	4
toy	1	3	3	2	3	3	1	2	3	3	4	1	3	4
waste	3	3	3	2	7	4	5	3	4	4	2	2	3	5

The table is read thus: Shorthand system No. 1 requires two strokes to write the word "abroad," shorthand system No. 2 requires three strokes, shorthand system No. 3 requires four strokes, shorthand system No. 4 requires two strokes, etc.

24

Table III

Extent to Which Shorthand Systems Abbreviate Words in Writing

Shorthand System	Outlines fully complete	Outlines more than half but not fully complete	Outlines half or less than half complete
1	0	1	23
2	7	11	6
3	No data		
4	12	9	3
5	11	10	3
6	8	7	9
7	No data		
8	No data		
9	8	7	9
10	No data		
11	21	2	1
12	9	10	5
13	No data		
14	No data		

The table is read thus: In a random sample of twenty-four words, shorthand system No. 1 does not write any word fully complete, one word is written more than half complete, and twenty-three words are written half or less than half complete.

Table II, based on a random sample of twenty-four words, indicates that there is a variation among the shorthand systems with respect to the writing of outlines representing the same longhand word. This variation indicates that some systems are more efficient than others with respect to the writing of outlines. A system in which a word can be written with one stroke would have greater writing efficiency than a system which requires five or six strokes.

3. In some systems words are written in such form that all the spoken sounds are represented, while other systems abbreviate the word which, of necessity, requires the reader to supply the unexpressed portion of the word. Table III (page 25) shows the extent to which shorthand systems abbreviate words in writing.

Table III, based on a random sample of twenty-four words, shows through comparison that there is a difference in the amount of abbreviating used by one shorthand system as compared to the amount of abbreviating used in another system. A system which uses a great many abbreviated words would conceivably be less efficient in the characteristic of reading accuracy than a system which writes the words in full. A system in which words are written in full would be most efficient for reading, in that each word would be unmistakable. A system using abbreviations would rely more upon the student's memory and knowledge of the abbreviation for the correct word, while a completely written word could be reconstructed by the reader from the fundamental sounds. It is conceivable that the efficiency of a system would vary in relation to the amount of abbreviating used in the system.

With these three major findings, it was evident that some system of quantitative evaluation could be applied to any manually written system of writing, whether longhand or shorthand.

CHAPTER 4

DEVELOPMENT OF FORMULAS FOR QUANTITATIVE EVALUATION

1. BASIS FOR THE FORMULA FOR HOMONYMETIC-INTENSITY

As indicated in the preceding chapter, three major factors seem to lend themselves to quantitative treatment, each of which is important in measuring efficiency factors of a short-hand system. The first of these to be considered involves the fact that in many systems of shorthand one outline may stand for several different words. This characteristic will be designated "homonymetic-intensity."

It is evident that, if a shorthand system is written with a large number of words represented by the same outline, the memory-burden or judgment factor is materially greater than if the system has no outlines which can be read for more than one word. Table I (page 23) indicates the extent to which this factor differs from system to system.

In determining the factors of a formula for measuring judgment which must be used in determining which word to use out of a number of choices, it was assumed that a system which has no homonyms would represent a perfect system, and would be assigned the value of 1.

If a word of high frequency has a high homonymetic-intensity, it is evident that the reader of the system will have to make more judgments than if a word of low frequency has a high homonymetic-intensity. This necessitated including, as one of the factors of the formula, the frequency of use of the words in the sample in this study.

Not only is the reader of a shorthand system with a high homonymetic-intensity concerned with judgment, but he is also concerned with the burden placed upon his memory in recalling which word was dictated to him, and, further, in recalling all of the words for which the outline stands.

With these two concepts, namely, judgment and memory-burden, to be measured, a single formula expressing the efficiency factor of memory-burden and judgment was developed in the following terms: $E_m = \frac{\Sigma fh}{N}$, where "$E_m$" is the coefficient of efficiency, "f" is the frequency of use for a given word as listed in Horn's Basic Writing Vocabulary (25) from which the sample was selected, "h" is the number of words which an outline can represent, and "N" is the sum of the frequencies of use as given in Horn's Basic Writing Vocabulary (25).

A hypothetical case will serve to illustrate the working of this formula -- $E_m = \frac{\Sigma fh}{N}$. If a system has no outline that represents any other outline, then "h" becomes 1. By definition "N" = "Σf"; "$\Sigma f1$" = "Σf"; therefore, "$\frac{\Sigma f}{N}$" = 1. If every outline in a system stands for two words, "h" has a value of 2; therefore, "E_m" by definition would equal 2.

Example: Hypothetical System No. 1

Word	Shorthand Outline	Number of Words It Can Represent	f	fh
go		2	10,000	20,000
be		3	5,000	15,000
much		1	1,000	1,000
			16,000	36,000
			N	Σfh

Substituting in the formula, $E_m = \frac{\Sigma fh}{N}$,

$$E_m = \frac{36,000}{16,000} \text{ or } 2.25$$

Hypothetical System No. 2

Word	Shorthand Outline	Number of Words It Can Represent	f	fh
go		1	10,000	10,000
be		1	5,000	5,000
much		1	1,000	1,000
			16,000	16,000
			N	Σfh

Substituting in the formula, $E_m = \frac{\Sigma fh}{N}$,

$$E_m = \frac{16,000}{16,000} \text{ or } 1.$$

As a result of the above examples, it can be seen that Hypothetical System No. 2 is a more efficient system than Hypothetical System No. 1 with respect to the characteristic of
homonymetic-intensity. In the first system the reader is required to use more judgment and is subject to a greater memory-
burden than he is in the second system.

In order to demonstrate that this formula can be effectively
applied to any manually written system of shorthand, data from
the materials received from the authors and writers were compiled for the ten systems which furnished data with regard to
this factor.

The specific steps involved in the final computation of
homonymetic-intensity are as follows:

1. To the right of each word of the 614 words of the random sample was written the weighted frequency of the word as
given in Horn's Basic Writing Vocabulary (25) (see Appendix
C).

Example: If Horn showed a frequency of 4,230 for the word
    "accept," 787 for "added," and 91,568 for "all,"
    the table appeared thus:
      accept   4,230
      added   787
      all   91,568, etc.

2. The next step was to add all of the 614 numbers representing the weighted frequency as given by Horn in his Basic
Writing Vocabulary (25). This summation of frequencies gave
the value for "N" in the formula to be used in evaluating
shorthand systems for the sample of the first three thousand
words. Since the same sample of words was used for all systems,
"N" became a constant factor in the formula. The value of "N"
was found to be 3,571,640.

3. The next step was to determine the value for "Σfh" for
each system. On the data sheets returned by the authors and
writers underneath each longhand word there appeared a small
Arabic number which represented the homonymetic-intensity of
the shorthand outline representing that word.

Example: (the longhand word) ANY (frequency as
      (homonymetic-intensity) 2   given in Horn) 51,010

The frequency, 51,010, was multiplied by 2. This was carried out cumulatively for each of the 614 words to find the value "Σfh" in the formula to be used in evaluating shorthand systems on the basis of a sample of the three thousand words. The actual value for "Σfh" was found to be 7,547,386 on the data representing shorthand system No. 1. This operation was carried out individually for each set of data sent in by the authors and writers.

4. The final step in evaluating the shorthand systems on the three thousand word level for this principle of evaluation was simply a matter of applying the values obtained for each shorthand system to the formula.

Example: The formula for determining the coefficient of efficiency for the principle of memory-burden and judgment is

$$E_m = \frac{\Sigma fh}{N}.$$

Substituting the values derived from the data for shorthand system No. 1,

$$E_m = \frac{7,547,386}{3,571,640} \text{ or } 2.1131.$$

Table IV (page 31) shows the coefficients of efficiency for homonymetic-intensity for the ten shorthand systems. These coefficients were obtained by applying the formula in the manner described above to each of the systems.

Table IV indicates that shorthand system No. 5 has no outline in the sample used in this study which stands for more than one word. On the other hand, system No. 1 has some words of high frequency which are represented by symbols that stand for more than two words. In other words, the reader of shorthand system No. 1 is required to make 2.1131 as many judgments in reading as is a reader of shorthand system No. 5.

The shorthand systems are listed in the table in order of rank, running from most efficient to least efficient, according to the coefficients of efficiency. Each system is designated by a number rather than by the actual name of the system for reasons which are explained immediately following.

In considering the tables which show coefficients of efficiency, three facts must be remembered. First, it is not the purpose of this study to evaluate shorthand systems, but to establish the principles for evaluating certain efficiency

factors. Second, by submitting the sample of words to authors
and expert writers it was discovered that some of these persons did not complete the necessary requirements for all three
principles of evaluation and it was therefore impossible to
compare all of the shorthand systems on each of the three principles. Third, inasmuch as it was impossible to obtain a sufficient number of experts to check the data submitted by authors
and writers, it was impossible to verify the accuracy of claims
for homonymetic-intensity and word-completeness factors.

Table IV

Coefficients of Efficiency Obtained for Homonymetic-Intensity
by Applying the Formula $E_m = \dfrac{\Sigma fh}{N}$ to a

614 Word Random Sample of Horn's
Three Thousand Words (25)

Shorthand System	Coefficient of Efficiency for Homonymetic-Intensity
5	1.0000
7	1.2246
3	1.2258
13	1.5029
4	1.5563
9	1.7213
2	1.8855
6	1.9756
8	2.0951
1	2.1131

The table is read thus: Shorthand system No. 5 ranks first
in efficiency with respect to the factor of homonymetic-
intensity, system No. 7 ranks second, system No. 3 ranks third,
etc.

Any author or inventor of a system of shorthand using the techniques and word sample herein demonstrated would be required to submit complete evidence regarding each of these factors in order to validate his claim for efficiency. This study did not set out to establish the claim for efficiency for any one system over another, but rather to indicate techniques which might be used for such evaluation.

The Application of the Formula to Words of High and Low Frequency

As indicated in the preceding chapter on the selection of a sample, a further study was made of the relative homonymetic efficiency of high-frequency words as compared to the homonymetic efficiency of words of low frequency. In computing the coefficients of efficiency for the word samples representing the highest frequency five hundred words and the lowest frequency five hundred words, the same mechanical operations were used as were used in applying the formula to a word sample of Horn's three thousand words.

Table V (page 33) indicates that, regardless of the frequency of words in these samples, the systems tend to fall in the same relative position with regard to homonymetic efficiency, whether the sample be chosen from words of high frequency or from words of low frequency.

Table V shows that every system in the group studied, with the exception of system No. 5, has a greater homonymetic-intensity for words of high frequency than for words of low frequency. It will be noted, however, that the degree of difference in the coefficient of efficiency for homonymetic-intensity between high- and low-frequency words is less in some systems than in others. For example: In the case of system No. 8 the coefficient of homonymetic efficiency for high-frequency words is 2.1211 and for low-frequency words it is 1.3286, $\frac{2.1211}{1.3286} = 1.596$; while in the case of system No. 7 the coefficient of efficiency for homonymetic-intensity for high-frequency words is 1.3231 and for low-frequency words it is 1.0128, $\frac{1.3231}{1.0128} = 1.306$.

In order to determine the degree of relationship between the coefficient of efficiency for homonymetic-intensity for high-frequency words as compared to the coefficients of efficiency for low-frequency words, a coefficient of correlation was computed and the product-moment r was found to be .80. This is greater than .76, which corresponds to P = .01, which means that there is less than one chance in a hundred that such a high coefficient of correlation could occur by chance.

Table V

Coefficients of Efficiency Obtained for Homonymetic-Intensity by Applying the Formula $E_m = \frac{\Sigma fh}{N}$ to a Random Sample of the Five Hundred Highest Frequency Words and a Sample of the Five Hundred Lowest Frequency Words of Horn's Three Thousand Words (25)

Shorthand System	Coefficient of Efficiency for High Frequency Words	Shorthand System	Coefficient of Efficiency for Low Frequency Words
5	1.0000	5	1.0000
7	1.3231	7	1.0128
9	1.6084	3	1.1599
13	1.6093	4	1.2366
3	1.7269	13	1.2600
4	1.7676	9	1.2866
6	1.9666	2	1.2977
2	2.0162	6	1.3022
1	2.1038	8	1.3286
8	2.1211	1	1.6710

The table is read thus: Shorthand system No. 5 ranks first in efficiency for homonymetic-intensity with respect to a sample of the five hundred highest frequency words, and it ranks first with respect to a sample of the five hundred lowest frequency words.

In view of the above facts, it is evident that it is need-less to evaluate shorthand systems separately on the basis of high- and low-frequency words with respect to homonymetic-intensity. The systems tend to maintain their same relative positions both on high-frequency words and on low-frequency words.

2. BASIS FOR THE FORMULA FOR WRITING EFFICIENCY

The second factor to be treated is writing efficiency. It arises from the fact that, among the several systems of short-hand, writing movement is employed in varying degrees for the writing of a single longhand word. If one shorthand system uses only one stroke for the writing of a word while another system requires four strokes to write the same word, the writ-ing efficiency is materially greater in the first system than in the second.

Table II (page 24) indicates the extent to which this factor has a bearing on the problem.

In determining the factors of a formula for measuring writing efficiency, it was assumed that a system which has only one writing stroke for each word would represent a perfect system and would be assigned the value of 1.

If a word of high frequency requires a large number of writ-ing strokes, it is evident that the writer of the system will need to make more writing movements than if a word of low fre-quency has a large number of writing strokes. This necessitated including, as one of the factors of the formula, the frequency of use of the words in the sample in this study.

These considerations point to the fact that writing efficien-cy can be quantitatively measured. Thus to measure writing ef-ficiency the following formula was developed: $E_w = \dfrac{\Sigma f S_1}{N}$, where "$E_w$" is the coefficient of efficiency for writing, "f" is the frequency of use for a given word as listed in Horn's Basic Writing Vocabulary (25) from which the sample was selected, "S_1" is the number of writing strokes taken to write an outline according to the principles of the system, and "N" is the sum of the frequencies of use as given in Horn's Basic Writing Vo-cabulary (25).

A hypothetical case will serve to illustrate the working of this formula, $E_w = \frac{\Sigma fS_1}{N}$. If a system writes every outline with a single stroke, then "S_1" becomes 1. By definition "N" = "Σf"; "$\Sigma f1$" = "Σf"; therefore, $\frac{\Sigma f}{N}$ = 1. If every word in a system is written with two strokes, "S_1" has a value of 2; therefore by definition "E_w" would equal 2.

Example: Hypothetical System No. 1

Word	Shorthand Outline	Number of Writing Strokes	f	fS$_1$
go		1	10,000	10,000
be		1	5,000	5,000
much		2	1,000	2,000
			16,000	17,000
			N	ΣfS_1

Substituting in the formula, $E_w = \frac{\Sigma fS_1}{N}$,

$E_w = \frac{17,000}{16,000}$ or 1.0625.

Hypothetical System No. 2

Word	Shorthand Outline	Number of Writing Strokes	f	fS$_1$
go		1	10,000	10,000
be		2	5,000	10,000
much		2	1,000	2,000
			16,000	22,000
			N	ΣfS_1

Substituting in the formula, $E_w = \frac{\Sigma fS_1}{N}$,

$E_w = \frac{22,000}{16,000}$ or 1.375.

It can be seen by the above example that Hypothetical System No. 1 is a more efficient system than Hypothetical System No. 2 for the characteristic of writing. In Hypothetical System No. 2 the writer would need to use more writing strokes than he would in Hypothetical System No. 1, which, in turn, would affect the efficiency of the system.

The steps involved in the final computation of the writing-efficiency factor are as follows:

1. To the right of each word of the 614 words of the random sample was written the weighted frequency of the word as given in Horn's **Basic Writing Vocabulary** (25).

Example: accept   4,230
           added   787
           all   91,568, etc.

2. "N" having been previously calculated for the formula of homonymetic-intensity, its value of 3,571,640 was used again in computing the writing-efficiency formula.

3. The next step was to determine the value for "$\Sigma f S_1$." This was done by counting the writing strokes of each shorthand outline as written according to the principles of the system, using the definition of <u>stroke</u> as set forth on page 2. The numbers representing the stroke count of each word was placed beside the shorthand outline.

Example: (the shorthand outline   (frequency
            written according to   as given
            principle)   by Horn)   51,010
            (the stroke count)   2

The frequency, 51,010, was multiplied by 2. This was carried out cumulatively for each of the 614 words to find the value of "$\Sigma f S_1$" in the formula to be used in evaluating shorthand systems on the basis of a sample of the three thousand words. The actual value for "$\Sigma f S_1$" was found to be 5,845,360 on the data representing shorthand system No. 1. This same process was carried out individually for each set of data sent in by the authors and writers.

4. The final step in evaluating the shorthand systems on a sample of three thousand words for the principle of writing efficiency was simply a matter of substituting the values obtained for the terms of the formula.

Example: The formula for determining the coefficient of efficiency for the principle of writing efficiency is

$$E_w = \frac{\Sigma f S_1}{N}.$$

Substituting the values derived from shorthand system No. 1 data,

$$E_w = \frac{5,845,360}{3,571,640} \text{ or } 1.6366.$$

Table VI (below) shows the coefficients of writing efficiency for the fourteen shorthand systems. These coefficients were obtained by applying the formula in the manner described above.

Table VI lists the shorthand systems in order of rank, running from most efficient to least efficient, according to the coefficients of efficiency obtained. Each system is designated by a number for reasons which have been explained above.

Table VI

Coefficients of Efficiency Obtained for Writing Efficiency by

Applying the Formula $E_w = \frac{\Sigma f S_1}{N}$ to a 614 Word Random Sample

of Horn's Three Thousand Words (25)

Shorthand System	Coefficient of Efficiency for Writing Efficiency
8	1.4974
12	1.4975
1	1.6366
2	1.7561
4	1.7583
11	1.9819
7	2.0020
3	2.0040
9	2.1411
10	2.1470
6	2.3209
13	2.5694
5	2.7419
14	3.4699

The table is read thus: Shorthand system No. 8 ranks first in writing efficiency, system No. 12 ranks second, etc.

The Application of the Formula to Words
of High and Low Frequency

As indicated in the preceding chapter on the selection of a
sample, a further study was made of the relative writing efficiency of high frequency words as compared to writing efficiency of words of low frequency.

In computing the coefficients of efficiency for the word
samples representing the highest frequency five hundred words
and the lowest frequency five hundred words, the same processes were used in computing the values for the terms of the
formula as were used in applying the formula to the sample of
Horn's three thousand words.

Table VII (page 39) indicates that, regardless of the frequency of words in these samples, the systems tend to fall in
the same relative position with regard to writing efficiency,
whether the sample be chosen from words of high frequency or
from words of low frequency.

Table VII shows that every system in the group studied shows
a higher stroke count for words of low frequency than for
words of high frequency. It will be noted, however, that the
degree of difference in number of strokes required to write
high-frequency words is less in some systems than in others.
For example: In the case of shorthand system No. 8 the coefficient of writing efficiency for high-frequency words is 1.4529
and for low-frequency words it is 2.7586, $\frac{2.7586}{1.4529} = 1.899$;
while in the case of system No. 5 the coefficient of writing
efficiency for high-frequency words is 2.6402 and for low-
frequency words it is 5.2851, $\frac{5.2851}{2.6402} = 2.002$.

In order to determine the degree of relationship between the
coefficients of efficiency for writing efficiency of high-
frequency words and the coefficients of efficiency for the
writing of low-frequency words, a coefficient of correlation
was computed and the product-moment r was found to be .92.
This was found to be greater than .66, which corresponds to
P=.01, which means that there is less than one chance in a
hundred that such a high coefficient of correlation could have
occurred by chance.

In view of the above facts it is evident that it is not

necessary to evaluate shorthand systems separately on the
basis of high- and low-frequency words with respect to writing
efficiency. The systems tend to maintain their same relative
positions on both high-frequency and low-frequency words.

Table VII

Coefficients of Efficiency Obtained for Writing Efficiency by
Applying the Formula $E_w = \frac{\Sigma f S_1}{N}$ to a Random Sample of the

Five Hundred Highest Frequency Words and a Sample of
the Five Hundred Lowest Frequency Words of
Horn's Three Thousand Words (25)

Shorthand System	Coefficient of Efficiency for High Frequency Words	Shorthand System	Coefficient of Efficiency for Low Frequency Words
12	1.3635	8	2.7586
8	1.4529	1	2.7817
1	1.4781	12	2.8057
2	1.6033	11	3.1777
4	1.6544	4	3.3245
11	1.7637	2	3.4928
7	1.8295	3	3.5804
9	2.0034	10	3.6639
3	2.0739	7	3.8337
10	2.2462	6	3.8677
6	2.2593	9	3.9175
5	2.6402	13	4.1955
13	2.6835	5	5.2851
14	3.3366	14	5.3376

The table is read thus: Shorthand system No. 12 ranks first
in writing efficiency with respect to a sample of the five
hundred highest frequency words, and it ranks third with respect to a sample of the five hundred lowest frequency words.

3. BASIS FOR THE FORMULA FOR WORD-COMPLETENESS

The third major factor to be considered is that of word-completeness. This involves the fact that, in many systems of shorthand, words are abbreviated instead of being sounded fully. This characteristic makes it necessary for the reader to identify the word either from memory of what was dictated, or from its association with the context in which it is written, or from a suggestion of the parts of the word which appear.

It is evident that a shorthand system in which all the sounds of each word are represented is more efficient than a system in which words are abbreviated. Table III (page 25) indicates the extent to which this factor has a bearing on the problem.

In determining the factors of a formula for measuring word-completeness, it was assumed that a system in which all words are fully represented in sound would represent a perfect system and would be assigned the value of 1.

If a word of high frequency is abbreviated, it is evident that the reader of the system will have to rely more often on memory or contextual material than he will if the abbreviation occurs in a word of low frequency. This necessitated including, as one of the factors of the formula, the frequency of use of the words in the sample in this study.

In order to show a sound in shorthand it is necessary to write something. Abbreviated words do not write the sounds which are left out; therefore, the difference in writing a fully sounded word and one which is abbreviated is represented by the amount of writing. The comparative difference would indicate the degree to which an outline is abbreviated.

These considerations point to the fact that word-completeness can be quantitatively measured; hence, the following formula was developed: $E_r = \dfrac{\Sigma f S_1}{\Sigma f S_2}$, where "$E_r$" is the coefficient of efficiency, "f" is the frequency of use for a given word as listed in Horn's Basic Writing Vocabulary (25), "S_1" is the number of writing strokes taken to write an outline according to the principles of the system, and "S_2" is the number of writing strokes taken to write an outline completely written according to spoken sounds.

A hypothetical case will serve to illustrate the working of this formula -- $E_r = \frac{\Sigma fS_1}{\Sigma fS_2}$. If a system writes every outline with one writing stroke and the completely written words require two strokes, then "E_r" will equal .5. By definition "E_r" equals $\frac{"\Sigma fS_1"}{\Sigma fS_2}$; if a system writes every outline with one stroke, then "S_1" becomes 1; therefore "Σf" equals "$\Sigma f1$." If it requires two strokes to write every word completely, then "S_2" becomes 2 and "$\Sigma f1$" divided by "$\Sigma f2$" equals .5; therefore "E_r" equals .5.

Example: Hypothetical System No. 1

Word	Shorthand Outline Written from Principle	Number of Writing Strokes	Shorthand Outline Written Completely	Number of Writing Strokes	f	fS_1	fS_2
go		1		2	10,000	10,000	20,000
be		1		2	5,000	5,000	10,000
much		2		3	1,000	2,000	3,000
					16,000	17,000	33,000
						ΣfS_1	ΣfS_2

Substituting in the formula, $E_r = \frac{\Sigma fS_1}{\Sigma fS_2}$,

$$E_r = \frac{17,000}{33,000} \text{ or } .5151$$

Hypothetical System No. 2

Word	Shorthand Outline Written from Principle	Number of Writing Strokes	Shorthand Outline Written Completely	Number of Writing Strokes	f	fS_1	fS_2
go		2		2	10,000	20,000	20,000
be		2		2	5,000	10,000	10,000
much		2		3	1,000	2,000	3,000
					16,000	32,000	33,000
						ΣfS_1	ΣfS_2

Substituting in the formula, $E_r = \dfrac{\Sigma fS_1}{\Sigma fS_2}$,

$$E_r = \frac{32,000}{33,000} \text{ or } .9696.$$

It can be seen by the above example that the outlines as written according to principle are more complete in Hypothetical System No. 2 than in Hypothetical System No. 1. This would indicate that the reader must rely more heavily upon memory or judgment in System No. 1 than he does in System No. 2; therefore, System No. 2 is more efficient with respect to the factor of reading.

The steps involved in computing the coefficients of efficiency for the word-completeness factor are as follows:

1. To the right of each word of the 614 words of the random sample was written the weighted frequency of the word as given in Horn's Basic Writing Vocabulary (25).

Example: accept 4,230
          added   787
          all   91,568, etc.

2. Having already determined "ΣfS_1" for the formula for writing efficiency, it was not necessary to compute it again. The value for "ΣfS_1" is 5,845,360 for shorthand system No. 1.

3. The final value to be obtained from each system in order to complete the formula was that of "ΣfS_2. This time the strokes were counted for each outline on the list of 614 words written according to the instructions for word-completeness. When this was done for each word in each shorthand system, the frequency for each word was multiplied by the number of strokes required to write that shorthand outline with word-completeness. The multiplication was cumulated for the 614 words and the resultant total for each shorthand system gave the value for "ΣfS_2." The actual value for "ΣfS_2" for shorthand system No. 1 is 16,449,940.

4. The final step in evaluating the shorthand systems on the three thousand word level for the principle of word-completeness was simply a matter of substituting the values obtained for each shorthand system in the formula.

Example: The formula for determining the coefficient of efficiency for the principle of word-completeness or reading accuracy is

$$E_r = \frac{\Sigma fS_1}{\Sigma fS_2}.$$

Substituting the values derived from shorthand system No. 1 data,

$$E_r = \frac{5,845,360}{16,449,940} \text{ or } .3553.$$

Table VIII (below) shows the coefficients of efficiency for the eight shorthand systems which furnished data on the word-completeness factor. These coefficients were obtained by applying the formula in the manner described above.

Table VIII

Coefficients of Efficiency Obtained for Word-Completeness by Applying the Formula $E_r = \frac{\Sigma fS_1}{\Sigma fS_2}$ to a 614 Word Random Sample

of Horn's Three Thousand Words (25)

Shorthand System	Coefficient of Efficiency for Word-Completeness
11	.9606
4	.8811
6	.7940
12	.7659
5	.7641
2	.6612
9	.6578
1	.3553

The table is read thus: Shorthand system No. 11 ranks first in efficiency with respect to the factor of word-completeness, system No. 4 ranks second, etc.

The Application of the Formula to Words
of High and Low Frequency

As indicated in Chapter III on the selection of a sample, a further study was made of the relative word-completeness efficiency of high-frequency words as compared to the word-

completeness efficiency of words of low frequency. In computing coefficients of efficiency for word samples representing
the five hundred highest frequency words and the five hundred
lowest frequency words, the same processes were applied in
computing the values for the terms of the formula as those
used in applying the formula to a sample of Horn's three thousand words.

Table IX (below) indicates that, regardless of the frequency
of words in these samples, the systems tend to fall in the
same relative position with regard to word-completeness, whether the sample be chosen from words of high frequency or from
words of low frequency.

<u>Table IX</u>

Coefficients of Efficiency Obtained for Word-Completeness by
Applying the Formula $E_r = \dfrac{\Sigma fS_1}{\Sigma fS_2}$ to a Random Sample of the

Five Hundred Highest Frequency Words and a Sample of
the Five Hundred Lowest Frequency Words of
Horn's Three Thousand Words (25)

Shorthand System	Coefficient of Efficiency for High Frequency Words	Shorthand System	Coefficient of Efficiency for Low Frequency Words
11	.8991	11	.9918
4	.8951	5	.8918
5	.7995	4	.8872
12	.7806	12	.8734
6	.7703	6	.7354
2	.6581	9	.7073
9	.6424	2	.7067
1	.3466	1	.3837

The table is read thus: Shorthand system No. 11 ranks first
in efficiency for word-completeness with respect to a sample
of the five hundred highest frequency words, and it ranks
first with respect to a sample of the five hundred lowest frequency words.

Table IX shows that all but two of the shorthand systems in
the group studied show greater word-completeness for words of
low frequency than for words of high frequency. It will be
noted, however, that the degree of comparative difference in
word-completeness required to write high-frequency words is
less in some systems than in others. For example: In the case
of system No. 11 the coefficient of efficiency for word-completeness for high-frequency words is .8991, and for low frequency words it is .9918, $\frac{.9918}{.8991}$ = 1.103; while in the case of
system No. 1 the coefficient of efficiency for word-completeness for high-frequency words is .3466 and for low-frequency
words it is .3837, $\frac{.3837}{.3466}$ = 1.107.

In order to determine the degree of relationship between the
coefficients of efficiency for word-completeness for high-
frequency words and the coefficients of efficiency for word-
completeness of low-frequency words, a coefficient of correlation was computed and the product-moment r was found to be .97.
This was found to be greater than .83, which corresponds to P =
.01, which means there is less than one chance in a hundred
that such a high coefficient of correlation could occur by
chance.

In view of the above facts it is evident that it is not necessary to evaluate shorthand systems separately on the basis
of high- and low-frequency words with respect to word-completeness. The systems tend to maintain their same relative positions on both high- and low-frequency words.

4. COMBINING THE FORMULAS TO OBTAIN A SINGLE COEFFICIENT
OF EFFICIENCY

Table IV (page 31) shows that shorthand system No. 5 ranks
the highest for the coefficient of efficiency of homonymetic-
intensity, Table VI (page 37) shows the same system next to
the bottom of the list with respect to the coefficient of efficiency for writing, and Table VIII (page 43) shows that for
word-completeness it is fifth from the top.

With this evidence it can be seen that a single coefficient
of efficiency which would express the general over-all efficiency of a system would be valuable. In order to obtain this
single coefficient, the major problem for consideration would

be the relative importance of each of the three principles of
evaluation presented here so that each might be weighted and
combined in a formula to give a single coefficient of efficiency. This is a problem for further research.

In the absence of any scientific research with respect to
the relative importance of each of the principles of evaluation presented here, the indices were combined without weighting to determine a coefficient of efficiency for the purpose
of illustrating the possibility of getting a representative
over-all coefficient of efficiency.

Example: $$E = \frac{\Sigma fh}{N} + \frac{\Sigma fS_1}{N} - \frac{\Sigma fS_1}{\Sigma fS_2}$$

To exemplify further these formulas combined into a single
formula, Table X (below) presents the combined coefficients of
efficiency for the six systems which returned data on all three
principles of evaluation. The coefficients of efficiency are
given in rank order from most efficient to least efficient as
obtained by combining the three principles of evaluation.

Table X

Coefficients of Efficiency Obtained for the Over-All Efficiency
of Each System by Applying the Combined Formula
$$E = \frac{\Sigma fh}{N} + \frac{\Sigma fS_1}{N} - \frac{\Sigma fS_1}{\Sigma fS_2}$$ to a 614-Word

Random Sample of Horn's Three
Thousand Words (25)

Shorthand System	Coefficient of Efficiency for Over-All Efficiency
4	2.4335
5	2.9778
2	2.9804
9	3.2046
1	3.3944
6	3.5025

The table is read thus: Shorthand system No. 4 ranks first in
efficiency for over-all efficiency as measured by a sample of
Horn's three thousand words.

Treated as though each factor of evaluation is equally
significant, the first two factors are added and the third
subtracted from the sum of the first two to get "E," which
represents, by and large, an over-all coefficient of efficiency. It might be said of "E" that, considering the structural
characteristics as represented by the three principles of evaluation, the system showing an "E" value nearest to +1.00 would
be the best shorthand system.

> Example: If it were possible for a shorthand system to be
> ideal, each factor would equal 1, as illustrated
> previously in this chapter. Combining the three
> factors, "E" for an ideal system would have a value
> of +1.00:

$$\frac{\Sigma fh}{N} + \frac{\Sigma fS_1}{N} - \frac{\Sigma fS_1}{\Sigma fS_2} = E; \text{ or}$$

$$1 + 1 - 1 = 1.$$

Using the six shorthand systems for which data were returned
for all three factors of evaluation, the following table further illustrates the relative position of each system for each
factor of evaluation as well as the relative position of the
system upon the over-all coefficient of efficiency.

Table XI

Shorthand Systems Arranged in Order of Rank for the Factors of
Homonymetic-Intensity, Writing Efficiency, Word-Completeness,
and the Combination of All Three According to
the Formula Used in Table X

Homonymetic Intensity	Writing Efficiency	Word Completeness	Combined Formula
5	1	4	4
4	2	6	5
9	4	5	2
2	9	2	9
6	6	9	1
1	5	1	6

CHAPTER 5

SUMMARY AND CONCLUSIONS

As a result of many claims to the superiority of one short-hand system over another made by authors and publishers, it was deemed valuable to develop a technique which can be used to prove or disprove such statements.

The purpose of this study is to isolate some of the factors which enter into the reading and writing of manually written shorthand systems, and, by considering these factors, to establish criteria for the objective evaluation of shorthand systems with respect to their facility of reading and writing.

PROCEDURE

A cursory study was made of several shorthand systems and it was found that shorthand systems, in general, have certain common characteristics which can be measured quantitatively.

As a result of this hypothesis, the following tentative assumptions were made:

1. A shorthand system in which any character represents the same word or phrase is more efficient than a system in which each character stands for more than one word.

2. A shorthand system in which there is a minimum of writing movements is more efficient than a system in which writing movements are numerous.

3. A shorthand system whose outlines completely express the longhand sounds is more efficient in reading than a system in which the sounds are abbreviated.

4. A shorthand system should use fewer writing movements for high-frequency words than it does for low-frequency words.

5. All shorthand systems use position.

In order to have a common basis upon which to test these assumptions, a representative sample of common English words was selected. This sample was made up of three random samples of words chosen from the first three thousand words in Horn's Basic Writing Vocabulary (25). The first sample was a five hundred word random sample taken from the entire list of three thousand words, the second was a seventy word random sample taken from the five hundred highest frequency words in Horn's three thousand, and the third was a seventy word random sample taken from the five hundred lowest frequency words in Horn's three thousand. When the three samples were combined and the duplicate words were eliminated, 614 words remained.

Since efficiency in shorthand is more important among words of high frequency and less important among words of low frequency, the weighted frequency as given in Horn's Basic Writing Vocabulary (25) was assigned to each of the 614 words. The two samples of seventy high-frequency words and seventy low-frequency words were taken for the purpose of determining whether or not there would be a significant difference in efficiency factors for high-frequency words as compared to the efficiency factors for words of low frequency.

These words were then submitted to authors and writers of several shorthand systems for the purpose of gathering data upon which to test the assumptions given above. When these data were received and tabulated, it became evident that the systems of shorthand vary among themselves, to a greater or less degree, in three major areas.

1. They vary with respect to the number of outlines which stand for more than one word. Table I (page 23) shows to what extent the systems vary. Because of this variance among the shorthand systems, it was conceived that there must be a variance of efficiency with respect to that characteristic in relation to the amount of that characteristic existing within a shorthand system. A student using a system containing homonyms must rely on memory or exercise judgment in determining the correct word. He must either remember the word dictated or recall all of the words that the outline may stand for and then, by reading the context surrounding the word, decide which is the correct word. It can readily be seen that a shorthand system having no homonyms would be the most efficient, because the necessity of memory-burden or the use of judgment would be eliminated.

2. There is a marked difference between the number of writing movements necessary for the same word in the various systems. Table II (page 24) indicates the extent to which this variation occurs. The indication is that some shorthand systems are more efficient with respect to writing efficiency than are others. A system in which each word may be written with one stroke would be more efficient than one in which five or six strokes are required.

3. There is a difference in the amount of abbreviation of words used by one system as compared to the amount of abbreviation used by another system. Table III (page 25) shows the extent to which this variation occurs. A system using abbreviations relies more upon the student's knowledge of the abbreviation for the correct word, while a completely written word can be reconstructed by the reader from the fundamental sounds. A system in which all of the words are written in full would be most efficient with respect to reading accuracy.

These three factors seemed to lend themselves to quantitative treatment, and each factor is important in measuring efficiency factors of a shorthand system. The first factor dealing with homonyms in shorthand is considered here as the factor of "homonymetic-intensity" and is measured by means of a formula which was developed in the following terms: $E_m = \frac{\Sigma fh}{N}$, where "$E_m$" is the coefficient of efficiency for homonymetic-intensity, "f" is the frequency of use for a given word as listed in Horn's Basic Writing Vocabulary (25) from which the sample was selected, "h" is the number of words which an outline can represent, and "N" is the sum of the frequencies of use given by Horn. A hypothetical case will serve to illustrate the formula. If, in one system, no outline represents more than one word, then "h" becomes 1. By definition "N" equals "Σf"; "$\Sigma f1$" equals "Σf"; therefore $\frac{\Sigma f}{N}$ equals 1. If in another system every outline stands for two words, "h" would have a value of 2, and "E_m" by definition would equal 2.

The data, which were collected from authors and writers of the several shorthand systems, consisted of the 614 words mentioned above. These words were returned with the number of homonyms marked for each word in the sample, a shorthand outline for each word in the sample written according to the principles of the system, and another shorthand outline written to to express all of the sounds in the longhand word. Ten authors or writers submitted data on homonyms, fourteen submitted data on the outlines written according to principle, and only eight submitted data for the completely written word. Six authors or writers completed all three factors for the data. Since it was impossible to obtain a sufficient number of experts to check the data submitted, it was impossible to verify the accuracy of the claims for homonymetic-intensity and word-completeness. However, it is not the purpose of this study to establish the claim for efficiency for any one system over another, but rather to indicate techniques involved.

The above formula was applied to these data, and coefficients of efficiency were computed for the factor of homonymetic-intensity. The coefficients were computed for the sample representing Horn's first three thousand words and also for the samples representing the five hundred highest frequency words and the five hundred lowest frequency words. The characteristic differences found among the coefficients of the last two samples were so small that making such a segregation of samples was needless. The same relative results were obtained by computing the coefficients upon the sample of the three thousand words. This fact holds true for all the factors of evaluation.

The second factor of efficiency is that of writing-efficiency, and it is measured by means of a formula developed in the following terms: $E_w = \dfrac{\Sigma f S_1}{N}$, where "$E_w$" is the coefficient of efficiency for writing efficiency, "f" is the frequency of use as given in Horn's Basic Writing Vocabulary (25) from which the sample was selected, "S_1" is the number of strokes required to write an outline according to principles, and "N" is the sum of the frequencies of use given by Horn. A hypothetical case will serve to illustrate the formula. If, in one system, each outline is written with only one stroke, then "S_1" becomes 1. By definition "N" equals "Σf"; "$\Sigma f 1$" equals "Σf"; therefore, "$\dfrac{\Sigma f}{N}$" equals 1. If, in another system, every outline was written with two strokes, "S_1" would have the value of 2, and "E_w" by definition equals 2.

The third factor of efficiency is the word-completeness factor, and it is measured by means of a formula developed in the following terms: $E_r = \frac{\Sigma fS_1}{\Sigma fS_2}$, where "$E_r$" is the coefficient of efficiency for word-completeness, "f" is the frequency of use as given in Horn's list, "S_1" is the number of strokes required to write an outline according to principles, and "S_2" is the number of strokes required to write a word when written with the completeness of longhand with respect to sound. A hypothetical case will serve to illustrate the formula. If, in one system, every outline is written with one stroke and the completely written words require the writing of two strokes, then "$\frac{\Sigma fS_1}{\Sigma fS_2}$" will equal .5. By definition "E_r" equals $\frac{\Sigma fS_1}{\Sigma fS_2}$". If a system writes every outline with one stroke, then "S_1" becomes 1, and therefore "$\Sigma f1$" equals "Σf." If it requires two strokes to write every word completely, then "S_2" becomes 2, and "$\Sigma f1$" divided by "$\Sigma f2$" equals .5; therefore "E_r" would equal .5.

When the coefficients of efficiency for the three factors of evaluation were determined, it was observed that no shorthand system consistently holds its relative position in efficiency for all three factors. By means of combining the three formulas, a single coefficient of efficiency can be computed. In the absence of research on the problem of weighting the factors to be combined, the factors were combined as having equal weight and it was discovered that a single over-all coefficient of efficiency is possible. The formula representing the over-all coefficient of efficiency is as follows: $E = \frac{\Sigma fh}{N} + \frac{\Sigma fS_1}{N} - \frac{\Sigma fS_1}{\Sigma fS_2}$. To discover the proper values with which to weight these factors is a problem for further research.

CONCLUSIONS

The purpose of this study was to establish principles for evaluating certain efficiency factors of shorthand systems. As a result of a cursory study certain assumptions were made to the effect that shorthand systems have certain common characteristics. These characteristics are set forth in the assumptions in Chapter III which point out that a shorthand system is efficient to the extent that its outlines represent only one word, it is efficient to the extent that a minimum of writing movement is necessary to write an outline, it is efficient to the extent that an outline is written to contain the complete longhand sounds, it is efficient to the extent that the greatest efficiency is exercised among the highest frequency words, and further it is assumed that all systems require position of strokes in relation to a line of writing.

As a result of a more comprehensive study of fourteen shorthand systems it was found that the characteristics mentioned above can be measured quantitatively, and formulas were developed and applied to demonstrate the fact.

The conclusions drawn from this study are as follows:

1. Shorthand systems have certain characteristics which are common to all systems.

2. Among these characteristics are three major factors, each of which can be quantitatively measured by applying the formulas presented in this study.

3. The first factor of efficiency is based upon the presence of homonyms in a shorthand system, which necessitates the exercise of memory and judgment by the reader of that system.

4. The second factor of efficiency is writing efficiency.

5. The third factor of efficiency is word-completeness. That is, a system which abbreviates words is not so efficient from a reading standpoint as a system in which words are fully written.

6. Efficiency among high-frequency words is more important than it is among words of low frequency.

7. Every shorthand system utilizes position with respect to the line of writing.

8. Since variations of rank in efficiency remain slight when high-frequency and low-frequency words are compared, it is needless to compare shorthand systems on separate samples of words.

9. A method of combining the three major factors of comparison can be accomplished by combining the formulas used to compute their coefficients of efficiency, assuming that each factor has equal weight. This problem needs further research.

10. In view of the fact that a procedure has been developed for the relative evaluation of shorthand systems, authors and owners of shorthand systems should strive to base their claims for the superiority of their system upon scientific methods of evaluation.

SUGGESTIONS FOR FURTHER RESEARCH

A. Further research is needed on the problem of stroke joinings. The method used in joining strokes within a shorthand character needs further study in order to determine the relative efficiency, with respect to writing, of certain types of joinings.

B. Further research is needed on the problem of homonymetic-intensity among certain strokes in shorthand. In the present study homonymetic-intensity is measured for words or characters in the various shorthand systems. There are, however, individual strokes within some systems which stand for more than one sound and thus require judgment in choosing the correct sound.

C. Further research is needed on the problem of efficiency of writing certain syllables and sounds in relation to their frequency of use. Frequently used sounds should be written with the greatest of efficiency.

D. Further research is needed on the problem of using single strokes to represent prefixes, suffixes, and other combinations of sounds. These add to the memory-burden, and further research may determine whether or not they affect reading accuracy.

E. Further research is needed to determine the relative importance of each of the principles of evaluation presented in the present study so that they may be weighted and combined to give a single over-all coefficient of efficiency for each shorthand system.

F. Further research is needed on the problem of relating the physical construction and characteristics of each shorthand system to the psychology of learning so that shorthand can be evaluated upon the principle of learning efficiency.

BIBLIOGRAPHY

Note: These references are referred to by the following numbers in the text.

1. Abernethy, L. S. Abernethy Curve Stroke Shorthand. Hollis: The author, 1928.
2. Barnhart, Earl W. An Analysis of the Work of a Stenographer. New York: Gregg Publishing Company, 1927. P. 17.
3. Betts, M. Elinor. "A Comparative Study of the Time Required for Development of Speed in Gregg Shorthand and Speedscript Shorthand." Master's Thesis, University of Pittsburgh, Pittsburgh, Pa., 1942.
4. "Biennial Survey of Education in the United States, 1934 to 1936," Bulletin Number 2. Washington, D. C. United States Government Printing Office (1937), 21.
5. Blackstone, E. G. "Commercial Education Research Abstracts," Business Education World, XIV (April, 1934), 507-09.
6. Brady, Marshall James. "An Exploratory Study of Student Performance in Beginning Gregg and Thomas Shorthand." Master's Thesis, University of Stanford School of Education, California, 1940.
7. Byrne, H. E. Byrne Simplified Shorthand. San Francisco: Byrne Publishing Company, 1935.
8. Chandler, Walter. Speedhand. Denver: The author, 1924.
9. Deemer, Walter L., and Rulon, Phillip J. An Experimental Comparison of Two Shorthand Systems. Harvard Studies in Education, XXVIII. Cambridge: Harvard University Press, 1942. P. 4.
10. Dettmann, F. O. Phonetic Shorthand. New York: The author, 1937.
11. Dewey, Godfrey. Relativ Frequency of English Speech Sounds. Harvard Studies in Education. Cambridge: Harvard University Press, 1923. P. 17.
12. Dewey, Godfrey. Script Shorthand. Lake Placid Club: General Shorthand Corporation, 1938.

13. Dickinson, J. B. Dickinson Shorthand. Louisville, Kentucky: Dickinson Publishing Company, 1931.

14. Fisher, R. A., and Yates, F. Statistical Tables for Biological, Agricultural, and Medical Research. London: Oliver and Boyd, 1938. Pp. 82-87.

15. Fitzgerald, J. B. Munson Shorthand. Chicago: Lyons and Carnahan Publishing Company, 1934.

16. 5,000 Most-Used Shorthand Forms. New York: Gregg Publishing Company, 1931.

17. Forkner, Hamden L.; Osborne, Agnes E.; and O'Brien, James E. Correlated Dictation and Transcription. Boston: D. C. Heath and Company, 1940. P. v.

18. Francis, F. S. "Direction Shorthand" (mimeographed). Olympia, Washington: The author, 1928.

19. Freeman, F. N. The Handwriting Movement. Supplementary Educational Monographs, Vol. II, No. 3. Chicago: University of Chicago Press, 1918. Pp. 4-17.

20. Gaffin, Myrtle. "Facts Concerning the Extent of Withdrawals from Shorthand," Research Studies in Commercial Education. University of Iowa Monographs, Vol. V, pp. 113-17.

21. Garber, Osborne. "Analysis of Four Popular Shorthand Systems," (unpublished investigation, Long Beach, Calif).

22. _____. International Shorthand. Long Beach: Progressive Publishing Company, 1935.

23. Gregg, John Robert. The Story of Shorthand. New York: Gregg Publishing Company, 1941.

24. _____. Gregg Shorthand (Anniversary Edition). New York: Gregg Publishing Company, 1929.

25. Horn, Ernest. A Basic Writing Vocabulary -- 10,000 Words Most Commonly Used in Writing. Iowa City: College of Education, University of Iowa, 1926.

26. Hyenga, Henry. Hyenga Shorthand. Chicago: Joseph P. Degan Publishing Company, 1928.

27. Karam, A. S. The American Shorthand. Oklahoma City: Karam Textbook Company, 1936.

28. Myers, Ernest M. Myers Shorthand System. Indiana: The author, 1939.

29. Pearman, W. I., and Parker, B. Capitol Shorthand. New York: Capitol Publishing Company, 1942.

30. Pitman, Isaac. New Standard Course in Shorthand. New York: Isaac Pitman and Sons, 1930.

31. Reigner, Charles G. Rowe Shorthand. Baltimore: The H. M. Rowe Company, 1920.

32. "Results! A Story of Achievement with Thomas Natural Shorthand." New York: Prentice-Hall, Inc.

33. Ross, J. Walter. Speedscript. Wilmington: Speedscript Publishing Company, 1939.

34. Rowe, Clyde Eugene. The Writing of Infrequently Used Words in Shorthand. Teachers College, Columbia University, Contributions to Education, No. 869. New York: Bureau of Publications, Teachers College, Columbia University, 1943. P. 56.

35. Rulon, Phillip J. Summary of the Study. Cambridge: Harvard University Press, 1942.

36. Shamburger, J. I. Shamburger Easy Shorthand. Dallas: The author, 1910.

37. Spencer, L. C. Spencerian Shorthand. New Orleans: Spencer Publication Company, 1936.

38. Stautzenberger, W. H. Stautzenberger Shorthand. Toledo: The W. H. Stautzenberger Publishing Company, 1937.

39. "The Speedscripter." Wilmington: Speedscript Publishing Company, Spring, 1943, Vol. I, p. 4.

40. Thomas, Charles A. Thomas Natural Shorthand. New York: Prentice-Hall, 1938.

41. Volk, Joseph. Volk's Universal Shorthand. New York: The author, 1940.

42. "With Reference to Success in Business." New York: Pitman Publishing Corporation, undated, p. 9.

APPENDIX A

Mr. John Doe
Blank Publishing Company
Chicago, Illinois

Dear Mr. Doe:

Your very kind cooperation last March, when I was making a
preliminary survey of various shorthand systems, has led me to
make further study of the characteristics of shorthand systems.
I hope to be able to include some of these findings in a doc-
toral dissertation here at Teachers College, Columbia University. I am enclosing with this letter a brief summary of the
information obtained as a result of the above mentioned survey.
I thought you would be interested in the results of the ques-
tionnaire which you were so kind to answer.

I do not like to impose upon your good nature, but I would
appreciate receiving from you, as soon as possible, the attached list of words with the shorthand equivalents in your
system written exactly as they would be if a competent stenographer were writing them from dictation. In addition to this,
however, I would also like to have the words written out completely in shorthand. This second outline should include all
of the sounds or essential letters included in the longhand
word. By essential I mean all letters or sounds required for
the accurate identification of the word. Although you may use
position to express some letters in the second outline, it is
necessary to have all of the letters written in, and prefixes
like con should be written with the three sounds K̆-O-N, suffixes like ing should be spelled out fully. Thirdly, I would
like to have you indicate how many words one outline may stand
for. One outline might stand for several words or even words
and phrases. For example: has three meanings in Gregg Shorthand, be, by, but; has two meanings, tooth, or to the. I
would like to know the total number of meanings which a single
outline may have.

The following is how the attached list of words would be
filled out:

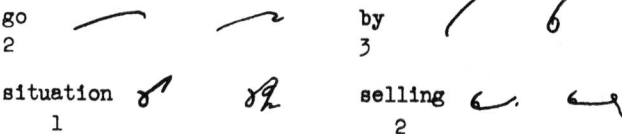

go
2

by
3

situation
1

selling
2

1. The shorthand outline as written when dictated.
2. The shorthand outline as written when spelled or sounded in
      full.
3. A small number under the longhand word to represent the num-
      ber of homonyms the first outline stands for.

The attached list of words is a random sampling of Ernest
Horn's first three thousand words. If this list does not include words which seem to exemplify some of the principles
which you feel are unique in your shorthand system, will you
be so kind as to list those words on the last sheet of the attached list and include the shorthand for them.

                              Sincerely,

APPENDIX B

A 614 WORD RANDOM SAMPLE OF THE FIRST THREE THOUSAND WORDS
OF ERNEST HORN'S LIST OF TEN THOUSAND
MOST FREQUENTLY USED WORDS

Example:

Longhand word	Shorthand as written from dictation	Shorthand as written when sounded in full
Consent		

1 - the number of meanings the first outline has.

Together		

4 - the number of meanings the first outline has.

Refer to Appendix C for the list of words referred to under
Appendix B.

APPENDIX C

KEY TO PHONETIC SPELLING

(i) as in Eat, lEE
(ɪ) as in hIt, tIn
(e) as in dEbris, locAte
(ɛ) as in mEt, tEn
(æ) as in hAt, tAn.
(a) as in dAnce, bAth
(ɑ) as in fAther, Odd
(ɒ) as in nOt, hOt
(ɔ) as in lAW, All
(ʌ) as in bUt, tUb
(o) as in Obey, tobaccO
(ʊ) as in pUll, fOOt
(u) as in fOOl, blUE
(ə) as in sofA, Account
(ər) as in buttER
(ɜr) as in bIRd, hER
(aɪ) as in Ice, AIsle
(aʊ) as in hOUse, bOUgh
(ɔɪ) as in OIl, vOId
(eɪ) as in lAte, mAIn
(oʊ) as in Old, snOw
(ju) as in YOU, fEUd
(jʊ) as in Unite
(b) as in Bird, criB
(d) as in Dip, baD
(f) as in Fine, leaF
(g) as in Go, eGG
(h) as in Ham, Humor
(j) as in Yes, Yet
(k) as in Count, Key

(l) as in Let, teLL
(m) as in Mad, daM
(n) as in Nod, maN
(p) as in Peace, PiP
(r) as in Red, dRip
(s) as in Cent, SitS
(t) as in Team, TighT
(v) as in Veil, driVe
(w) as in Watch, War
(z) as in Zero, buZZ
(ŋ) as in huNG, siNG
(ʃ) as in SHip, diSH
(ʒ) as in pleaSure, caSual
(θ) as in THin, widTH
(ð) as in THine, liTHe
(hw) as in WHere, WHat
(tʃ) as in CHurCH, CHoose
(dʒ) as in Judge, Gem
(g) is always as in Go
(j) has the sound of "y,"
            "j," as in Jump
(s) and (z) are hissed as in
            ghoSt, goeS
(c) = "s" or "k" as in Cent,
            Crush
(q) = "kw" as in QUick
(x) = "ks" or "gs" as in
            eXpect, eXult
(y) = "j" as in Yacht

On the following pages will be found a 614 word sample of the first three thousand words of Horn's basic writing vocabulary including word, phonetic spelling, and frequency of use.

abroad	əbrɔd	223	attach	ətætʃ	456
accept	æksept; ə	4230	attend	ətend	1883
acceptance	æksəptəns	372	author	ɔθə(r)	413
actual	æktʃuəl	567	authority	əθɒrətɪ, 'ɑ	690
add	æd	2225	bag	bæg	628
added	ædɪd; əd	787	bags	bægz	221
administration	ə|ædmɪnəstreɪʃ(ə)n	297	balance	bæləns	7391
admire	ədmaɪə(r)	279	banks	bæŋks	302
admitted	ədmɪtɪd; əd	217	banking	bæŋkɪŋ	261
adopted	ədɒptɪd; ɑ; —əd	531	barn	bɑ(r)n	237
advised	ədvaɪzd	2886	base	beɪs	370
affection	əfɛkʃ(ə)n	217	bat	bæt	282
after	æftə(r)	23016	basketball	bæskɪtbɔl; kət	366
agent	eɪdʒ(ə)nt	1599	be	bi	147612
all	ɔl	91568	beach	bitʃ	265
almost	ɔlmoʊst	4538	bear	bɛə(r)	1271
always	ɔlwɪz	10874	beautiful	bjutəfəl	2496
ambition	æmbɪʃ(ə)n	293	become	bɪkʌm; bə	1865
amount	əmaʊnt	11873	bee	bi	267
anticipate	æntɪsəpeɪt	259	beg	bɛg	4940
any	ɛnɪ	51010	began	bɪgæn, bə—	891
appeal	əpil	432	begins	bɪgɪnz; bə—	310
application	æplɪkeɪʃ(ə)n	2387	begun	bɪgʌn; bə—	350
approximately	əprɒksəmətlɪ; ɑ	514	being	biɪŋ	13658
aren't	ɑ(r)nt	378	belief	bɪlif, bə—	361
arrangement	əreɪndʒmənt	1648	belt	bɛlt	312
arrive	əraɪv	1052	beside	bɪsaɪd; bə—	429
article	ɑ(r)tɪkl	1550	bet	bɛt	628
ashamed	əʃeɪmd	652	between	bɪtwin; bə—	3848
asked	æskt	4985	birthday	bs(r)θdeɪ	1111
assigned	əsaɪnd	227	books	bʊks	4821
assist	əsɪst	779	both	boʊθ	7614
assistance	əsɪst(ə)ns	1155	borrow	bɒroʊ	263
assume	əs(j)um	997	branch	bræntʃ	691

Word	Pronunciation	Freq
breaking	breɪkɪŋ	230
bring	brɪŋ	5537
brother	brʌðə(r)	1977
brothers	brʌðə(r)z	253
buildings	bɪldɪŋz	246
busy	bɪzɪ	4585
cake	keɪk	712
cannot	kænɒt; nat	11634
can't	kænt	4246
capacity	kəpæsɪtɪ; -sə-	641
capital	kæpɪt(ə)l; -pə-	322
captain	kæptɪn; -t(ə)n	221
careful	keə(r)f(ʊ)l	3098
carefully	keə(r)fʊlɪ	1683
carrying	kærɪɪŋ	638
cars	ka(r)z	1612
case	keɪs	7855
caught	kɔt	560
caused	kɔzd	730
certainly	sɜ(r)t(ə)nlɪ	6611
chairman	tʃeə(r)mən	474
chairs	tʃeə(r)z	225
chance	tʃæns	2910
chances	tʃænsɪz; -əz	288
changes	tʃeɪndʒɪz; -əz	969
chapter	tʃæptə(r)	487
charges	tʃa(r)dʒɪz; -əz	1950
cheer	tʃɪə(r)	226
chemistry	kemɪstrɪ	214
chickens	tʃɪk(ə)nz	277
children	tʃɪldrən	3269
circumstances	sɜ(r)kəmstænsɪz; -əz	1356
city	sɪtɪ	6929
cleaned	klind	378
cleaning	klinɪŋ	246
clerk	klɜ(r)k	495
climate	klaɪmɪt; -ət	226
coats	kouts	271
collar	kɒlə(r); ka-	263
collection	kəlekʃ(ə)n	2256
college	kɒlɪdʒ; ka-	3362
come	kʌm	32588
community	kəmjunɪtɪ; -nə-	537
company	kʌmp(ə)nɪ	11276
compare	kəmpeə(r)	253
competition	kɒmpətɪʃ(ə)n; ka-	238
concert	kɒnsə(r)t; ka-	345
conclude	kənklud	250
connected	kənektɪd; -əd	467
consideration	kənsɪdəreɪʃ(ə)n	2546
constantly	kɒnstəntlɪ; ka-	243
could	kʊd	22101
cover	kʌvə(r)	5806
conversation	kɒnvə(r)seɪʃ(ə)n; ka-	926
cooperate	koupəreɪt; -ap-	449
correctly	kərektlɪ	321
council	kaʊns(ə)l	248
cousin	kʌz(ə)n	864
crazy	kreɪzɪ	1035
credits	kredɪts; -əts	269
current	kɜrənt	695
cutting	kʌtɪŋ	370
dances	dænsɪz; -əz	239
date	deɪt	10226
days	deɪz	9854
dealers	dilə(r)z	428
decision	dɪsɪʒ(ə)n; də-	913
deed	did	230

deep	dip	902
demands	dɪmændz; də-	216
department	dɪpɑ(r)tmənt; də-7028
deposit	dɪpɒzɪt; də-; ɑ; 501
desire	dɪzaɪə(r); də-	6273
detail	dɪteɪl; də-	709
developed	dɪvɛləpt; də-	321
die	daɪ	673
direct	dɪrɛkt; də-	3406
directed	dɪrɛktɪd; də-;-əd 342
directors	dɪrɛktə(r)z; də- 294
disappointed	dɪsəpoɪntɪd; -əd 1099
dispose	dɪspouz	611
divided	dɪvaɪdɪd; də; -əd 238
does	dʌz	5724
dollar	dʊlə(r); dɑ-	937
doubt	daʊt	4365
down	daʊn	11022
dozen	dʌz(ə)n	2260
dreams	drimz	241
dressed	drɛst	366
drink	drɪŋk	288
drive	draɪv	875
dry	draɪ	1114
dull	dʌl	248
easier	izɪə(r)	362
easy	izɪ	1313
editor	ɛdɪtə(r); -də-	238
effective	ɪfɛktɪv	544
eighteen	eɪtin	229
employees	ɛmploɪz	357
end	ɛnd	5091
engine	ɛndʒ(ə)n	295
enjoyed	ɛndʒoɪd; ɪn-	1269

enjoying	ɛndʒoɪɪŋ; ɪn-	698
enter	ɛntə(r)	1104
everyone	ɛvrɪwʌn	773
everything	ɛvrɪθɪŋ	4458
everywhere	ɛvrɪhwɛə(r)	233
exchange	ɛkstʃeɪndʒ; ɪk- 1414
exclusive	ɛksklusɪv; ɪk-	262
expecting	ɛkspɛktɪŋ; ɪk-	724
extending	ɛkstɛndɪŋ; ɪk-	229
extra	ɛkstrə	1904
fact	fækt	6999
family	fæm(ə)lɪ	2822
farm	fɑ(r)m	2087
fate	feɪt	213
favorably	feɪv(ə)rəblɪ	330
favorite	feɪv(ə)rət	289
feel	fil	12435
fence	fɛns	219
figured	fɪgjʊə(r)d	417
fill	fɪl	2186
filled	fɪld	1459
filling	fɪlɪŋ	673
finest	faɪnɪst; əst	277
folk	foʊk	301
followed	fɒloʊd	568
following	fɒloʊɪŋ	5382
fond	fɒnd; ɑ	241
foreign	fɒrɪn; fɑ-	913
forgotten	fəgɒt(ə)n; -gɑ-	845
formerly	fo(r)mə(r)lɪ	416
forty	fo(r)tɪ	589
forwarded	fowə(r)dɪd; -əd 2813
four	foə(r); oə	5723
found	faʊnd	5485

foundation	faʊndeɪʃ(ə)n	224	help	hɛlp	6111
Friday	fraɪdɪ	3848	helped	hɛlpt	647
friend	frɛnd	7931	her	hə(r)	42314
from	frʊm; ə	70382	here	hɪə(r)	39034
foot	fʊt	903	highest	haɪɪst; —əst	696
full	fʊl	4999	hills	hɪlz	245
funeral	fjunərəl	269	his	hɪz	26409
fur	fə(r)	1909	honest	ɒnɪst; ɑ—; —əst	794
furnish	fə(r)nɪʃ	4075	honor	ɒnə(r); ɑ	1103
further	fə(r)ðə(r)	6323	horses	hɔ(r)sɪz; —əz	355
furthermore	fə(r)ðə(r)mɔə(r)	247	hospital	hɒspɪt(ə)l; ɑ; —ɪə-947
game	geɪm	2151	hour	aʊə(r)	049
gave	geɪv	4037	household	haʊshould	263
genius	dʒinjəs	244	how	haʊ	28755
genuine	dʒɛnjʊɪn	240	human	hjumən	860
gets	gɛts	832	hurry	hərɪ	984
getting	gɛtɪŋ	7522	I'll	aɪl	363
give	gɪv	18820	I'm	aɪm	999
given	gɪv(ə)n	7399	if	ɪf	93437
gladly	glædlɪ	823	illness	ɪlnɪs; nəs	264
glass	glæs	832	importance	ɪmpo(r)təns	493
glorious	glorɪəs; glo—	554	improve	ɪmpruv	263
grandma	grændma	265	include	ɪnklud	1387
grateful	greɪtful	316	including	ɪnkludɪŋ	1603
gray	greɪ	536	independent	ɪndɪpɛndənt; —də— 264
guard	gɑ(r)d	283	individual	ɪndɪvɪdʒʊəl; —də— 601
hair	hɛə(r)	1375	influence	ɪnfluəns	564
half	hæf	3866	inquire	ɪnkwaɪə(r)	435
hands	hændz	2199	inquiry	ɪnkwaɪ(ə)rɪ	2205
happen	hæp(ə)n	1419	insist	ɪnsɪst	445
happy	hæpɪ	4773	inspection	ɪnspɛkʃ(ə)n	510
hay	heɪ	800	instant	ɪnstənt	1028
he	hi	65157	instead	ɪnstɛd	2942
heat	hit	370	instructions	ɪnstrʌkʃ(ə)nz	2654

insured	ɪnʃʊə(r)d	220	longer	lɒŋgə(r)	1768
intelligent	ɪntɛlɪdʒənt; -lə	241	looking	lʊkɪŋ	3981
inventory	ɪnvəntorɪ; -to-	360	love	lʌv	14434
investigate	ɪnvɛstɪgeɪt; -tə-	361	lover	lʌvə(r)	268
invitation	ɪnvəteɪʃ(ə)n	943	loves	lʌvz	295
invited	ɪnvaɪtɪd; -əd	883	luncheon	lʌntʃ(ə)n	265
iron	aɪə(r)n	817	machines	məʃinz	380
joy	dʒɔɪ	549	magazine	mægəzin	428
justified	dʒʌstɪfaɪd; -tə-	441	maid	meɪd	223
justify	dʒʌstɪfaɪ; -tə-	245	make	meɪk	25605
keen	kin	288	making	meɪkɪŋ	8234
keeps	kips	410	mamma	mɑmə	1007
kinds	kaɪndz	355	manner	mænə(r)	2028
king	kɪŋ	268	man's	mænz	380
know	noʊ	46680	manufacturers	mænjufæktʃərə(r)z	406
knows	noʊz	1212	many	mɛnɪ	11774
lading	leɪdɪŋ	733	married	mærɪd	2413
lake	leɪk	449	marry	mærɪ	347
land	lænd	2784	match	mætʃ	364
language	læŋgwɪdʒ	551	materials	mətɪ(ə)rɪəlz	327
largely	lɑ(r)dʒlɪ	235	matter	mætə(r)	18899
later	leɪtə(r)	3572	matters	mætə(r)z	2288
latter	lætə(r)	1551	me	mi	85505
laundry	londrɪ	248	mean	min	3421
leave	liv	5674	meant	mɛnt	799
leg	lɛg	470	meat	mit	258
leisure	liʒə(r)	222	medium	midɪəm	233
lies	laɪz	233	merely	mɪə(r)lɪ	1095
light	laɪt	2444	message	mɛsɪdʒ	636
list	lɪst	5850	methods	mɛθədz	436
listen	lɪs(ə)n	636	might	maɪt	8602
live	lɪv	2810	mill	mɪl	621
loads	loʊdz	220	mind	maɪnd	5572
located	loʊkeɪtɪd; -əd	864	minds	maɪndz	288

minimum	mɪnəməm	302	omitted	omɪtɪd; —əd	471
minutes	mɪnɪts; —əts	1485	on	ɒn; ɒ	100396
mistake	mɪsteɪk; mə—	1334	one	wʌn	66588
modern	mɒdə(r)n; mɑ	575	operated	ɒpəreɪtɪd; ɑ—;—əd	254
moment	moʊmənt	1700	operating	ɒpəreɪtɪŋ; ɑ—	337
month	mʌnθ	8148	opinion	əpinjən	2352
mood	mud	237	opinions	əpɪnjənz	233
more	moə(r)	21097	orchestra	ɔ(r)kəstr̩	295
mostly	moʊstlɪ	373	ordered	ɔ(r)də(r)d	3952
mother's	mʌðə(r)z	280	originally	ərɪdʒ(ə)nəlɪ	528
mountain	maʊnt(ə)n	273	outlined	aʊtlaɪnd	405
mountains	maʊnt(ə)nz	557	oversight	oʊvə(r)saɪt	344
must	mʌst	20002	own	oʊn	9325
movies	muvɪz	228	page	peɪdʒ	2141
my	maɪ	76257	pages	peɪdʒɪz; —əz	728
name	neɪm	7285	pan	pæn	298
namely	neɪmlɪ	360	papers	peɪpə(r)z	2590
nation	neɪʃ(ə)n	330	paragraph	pærəgræf	437
nature	neɪtʃə(r)	1486	parties	pɑ(r)tɪz	702
neighbor	neɪbə(r)	299	parts	pɑ(r)ts	1630
neighborhood	neɪbə(r)hʊd	308	pay	peɪ	9059
nice	naɪs	5736	peach	pitʃ	227
night	naɪt	13228	pen	pɛn	1191
nine	naɪn	1211	pencil	pɛns(ə)l	375
nothing	nʌθɪŋ	7770	perfect	pɜ(r)fɪkt	1239
notion	noʊʃ(ə)n	275	perfectly	pɜ(r)fɪktlɪ	1311
November	novɛmbə(r)	3298	perhaps	pə(r)hæps	4297
occasion	əkeɪʒ(ə)n	1289	permanent	pɜ(r)mənənt	463
occasional	əkeɪʒ(ə)nəl	220	piano	pɪæno	520
occupied	ɒkjupaɪd; ɑ—	218	pink	pɪŋk	254
off	ɒf	9688	planned	plænd	684
offices	ɒfɪsɪz; —fə—; —əz	387	plants	plænts	348
official	əfɪʃ(ə)l	597	plates	pleɪts	394
often	ɒf(ə)n	2872	poetry	poʊtrɪ	401

67

politics	pɒlɪtɪks; -pɑ-; lə	293
positions	pəzɪʃ(ə)nz	220
poultry	poʊltrɪ	261
pound	paʊnd	583
praise	preɪz	220
prepared	prɪpsə(r)d; prə-	1103
president	prɛzɪdənt; -zə-	2874
press	prɛs	450
previously	prɪvɪəslɪ	393
priced	praɪst	317
prices	praɪsɪz; -əz	5264
principles	prɪnsɪplz; -sə-	269
prior	prɑɪə(r)	425
private	praɪvɪt; -ət	782
prize	praɪz	331
production	prədʌkʃ(ə)n	386
professor	prəfɛsə(r)	372
program	progræm	1630
progress	prɒgrɪs; prɑ; -əs	489
promises	prɒmɪsɪz; ɑ -ə -ə	220
providing	prəvaɪdɪŋ	393
purchase	pɜ(r)tʃəs	2252
put	pʊt	11726
quantities	kwɒntətɪz; ɑ-	246
quarter	kwɔ(r)tə(r)	743
quotations	kwoteɪʃ(ə)n	374
quoted	kwoʊtɪd; -əd	688
rag	ræg	219
rapidly	ræpɪdlɪ; -pəd-	348
rather	ræðə(r)	6397
raised	reɪzd	258
reads	ridz	221
real	rɪəl	4624
realized	rɪəlaɪzd	255

reason	riz(ə)n	5446
reception	rɪsɛpʃ(ə)n; rə-	318
recommend	rɛkəmɛnd	1048
recommended	rɛkəmɛndɪd; -əd	307
refuse	rɪfjuz; -rə-	313
regarding	rɪgɑ(r)dɪŋ; rə-	7662
regards	rɪgɑ(r)dz; rə-	2152
regret	rɪgrɛt; rə-	4009
regretting	rɪgrɛtɪŋ; rə-	423
regular	rɛgjʊlə(r)	2929
release	rɪlis; rə-	283
reliable	rɪlaɪəbl; rə-	254
remains	rɪmeɪnz; rə-	359
remark	rɪmɑ(r)k; rə-	265
remarks	rɪmɑ(r)ks; rə-	288
remarkable	rɪmɑ(r)kəbl; rə-	246
remember	rɪmɛmbə(r); rə-	4715
remittance	rɪmɪtəns; rə-	4456
render	rɛndə(r)	419
report	rɪpɔə(r)t; rə-	5408
reported	rɪpɔə(r)tɪd; -əd	732
representatives	rɛprɪzɛntətɪvz; -prə-	367
represents	rɛprɪzɛnts; -prə-	326
requirements	rɪkwaɪə(r)mənts; rə-	1415
responsible	rɪspɒnsɪbl; rə-; -spɑn-; -sb-	440
returning	rɪtɜ(r)nɪŋ; rə-	4860
rise	raɪz	222
roads	roʊdz	545
roll	roʊl	252
roof	ruf	225
room	rum	5954
route	rut	423
rubber	rʌbə(r)	238
run	rʌn	4690

ush	rʌʃ	1031	shortly	ʃɔ(r)tlɪ	662
sale	seɪl	4016	showing	ʃoʊɪŋ	2252
salesman	seɪlzmən	609	shown	ʃoʊn	1782
sat	sæt	847	side	saɪd	3427
satisfaction	sætɪsfækʃ(ə)n; -təs-	1352	sight	saɪt	861
say	seɪ	27439	sing	sɪŋ	384
saying	seɪɪŋ	1642	single	sɪŋgl	1234
says	sɛz	2326	sixth	sɪksθ	213
scale	skeɪl	269	size	saɪz	4852
schools	skulz	851	skirt	sk ɜ(r)t	453
score	skoə(r)	292	small	smɔl	4552
season	siz(ə)n	2287	something	sʌmθɪŋ	7570
secretary	sɛkrɪtsrɪ; -rə-	1551	somewhat	sʌmhwɒt; ɑ	1310
section	sɛkʃ(ə)n	1047	speak	spik	2006
sections	sɛkʃ(ə)nz	351	specifications	spɛsɪfɪkeɪʃ(ə)nz; -əfə-	276
selected	sɪlɛktɪd; sə-;-əd	502	spent	spɛnt	1557
self	sɛlf	672	steady	stɛdɪ	240
sell	sɛl	2685	step	stɛp	666
sending	sɛndɪŋ	9133	stood	stʊd	414
sensible	sɛnsɪbl; sə-	244	stores	stoə(r)z	522
September	sɛptɛmbə(r)	1853	strange	streɪndʒ	728
sermon	s ɜ(r)mən	ˉ238	studying	stʌdɪɪŋ	917
service	s ɜ(r)vɪs; -əs	9515	style	staɪl	2547
serving	s ɜ(r)vɪŋ	645	subject	sʌbdʒɪkt	5080
settled	sɛtld	717	substitute	sʌbstɪt(j)ut; -stə-	421
settlement	sɛtlmənt	1845	sudden	sʌd(ə)n	274
seven	sɛv(ə)n	1620	suffer	sʌfə(r)	323
several	sɛv(ə)rəl	6158	sufficiently	səfɪʃ(ə)ntlɪ	244
severe	sɪvɪə(r); sə-	298	suggest	sə(g)dʒɛst	2858
shade	ʃeɪd	233	supplies	səplaɪz	577
sheets	ʃits	535	supply	səplaɪ	3764
shipped	ʃɪpt	4091	swell	swɛl	338
shock	ʃɒk; ɑ	267	teach	titʃ	1694
shoes	ʃuz	666	teacher	titʃə(r)	2396

tell	tɛl	10091	us	ʌs	47444
telling	tɛlɪŋ	1006	use	juz	14188
tender	tɛndə(r)	231	using	juzɪŋ	1520
term	tɜ(r)m	1037	vacation	vekeɪʃ(ə)n	2239
thanks	θæŋks	2123	views	vjuz	315
Thanksgiving	θæŋksgɪvɪŋ	225	visiting	vɪzɪtɪŋ; -zə-	604
that's	ðæts	352	visitor	vɪzɪtə(r); -zə-	225
there	ðɛə(r)	49501	walked	wokt	416
therefore	ðɛə(r)foə(r)	7036	war	wo(r)	3852
think	θɪŋk	27447	warrant	worənt	410
throughout	θruaʊt	494	wasn't	wɒznt; ɑ	765
tickets	tɪkɪts; —əts	272	waste	weɪst	4970
till	tɪl	1922	ways	weɪz	574
time	taɪm	66396	wearing	wɛərɪŋ	401
times	taɪmz	2665	weeks	wiks	3792
tired	taɪə(r)d	1561	weigh	weɪ	259
title	taɪtl	427	weight	weɪt	1272
to	tu	496776	were	wɜ(r)	32302
tomorrow	təmɒro; ɑ	3464	when	hwɛn	54326
toy	toɪ	219	whole	hoʊl	4175
track	træk	411	wholesale	hoʊlseɪl	236
traffic	træfɪk	332	whose	huz	1242
training	treɪnɪŋ	776	without	wɪðaʊt	9680
transferred	trænsfɜ(r)d	337	wish	wɪʃ	16137
treated	tritɪd; —əd	383	woman	wʊmən	1759
truth	truθ	1312	wonderful	wʌndə(r)ful	2848
truly	trulɪ	8793	wool	wʊl	254
try	traɪ	8943	word	wɜ(r̩)d	2757
type	taɪp	47444	world	wɜ(r)ld	4530
unfortunate	ʌnfo(r)tʃ(ə)nɪt; -ət	243	would	wʊd	55183
union	junjən	950	written	rɪt(ə)n	6478
until	ʌntɪl	13061	year	jɪə(r)	16438
up	ʌp	44584	yet	jɛt	11803
upper	ʌpə(r)	304	you	ju	338812
urge	ɜ(r)dʒ	274	youth	juθ	386

VITA

Marsdon Alexander Sherman was born in San Francisco, California, October 30, 1907. He received a B. A. degree from Stanford University in 1931 and an M. A. degree from the same university in 1942. He is the author of the following:

1. "An Exploratory Study of Certain Factors in the Prognosis of Achievement in Gregg Shorthand." An unpublished M. A. Thesis submitted to the School of Education, Stanford University, California, 1942.

2. "A Study of Prognosis in Shorthand," Business Education World, April, 1942, pp. 696-98.

3. "The Rule of 27," Business Education World, September, 1942, pp. 12-13.

4. "Factors in Stenographic Prognosis," The National Business Education Quarterly, October, 1942, pp. 37-38.

5. "A Filing Clinic," The Balance Sheet, November, 1942, pp. 116-17.

6. "Mortality in Beginning Stenography," The Journal of Business Education, December, 1942, pp. 17-18.

7. "Wartime Problems of Personal Adjustment from the Junior College Point of View," Sixth Yearbook, Eastern Commercial Teachers Association, 1943, pp. 67-73.

8. "Society for the Advancement of Research in Business Education Stimulates Research," Business Education World, September, 1944, p. 26.

9. "Shorthand Bingo," Business Education World, January, 1945, p. 271.

10. "Preparation and Professional Growth of Business Teachers," The Journal of Business Education, February, 1945, pp. 11-13.